Walks in
London

Caroline Swash

Connecting the buildings
where the most interesting
windows can be seen

MALVERN ARTS PRESS

The publication of this book has been made
possible with a grant from Central Saint Martins
College of Art & Design (The London Institute)

ISBN 0-9541055-0-8

Second Edition 2004
Published in 2002 by
Malvern Arts Press Ltd
PO Box 3
Malvern WR14 1WW
United Kingdom

Designed and set by Ginger Ferrell
in Arial, Garamond, Bradley Hand ITC
Printed in the UK by Aldine Print, Malvern

Every site has been revisited in 2001
for this publication. However, church openings
change over the years and shops and offices
change hands and use. I would be grateful for
any comments that would improve the usefulness
and interest of later editions.

Robert Eberhard and Peter Matthews have
assisted with corrections for this reprint.

**It is strongly advised that you bring
an A-Z map of London with you.**

Sketch maps by the author produced
by permission of
Geographers' A-Z Map Co Ltd.Licence No B1254
This product includes mapping data licensed from
Ordnance Survey®. ©Crown Copyright 2001.
Licence number 100017302

For Sheila Mole,
with whom this venture began

The walks take between 1 & 3 hours, start and finish in the following areas at an underground station.

14 walks

Stained glass should always be looked at in context. As an architectural art, it is best seen within the building for which it has been designed. London has a wonderfully rich and diverse heritage of stained glass in spite of the depredations caused by the Reformation, Great Fire and the bombing of London during the Second World War. Indeed the reconstruction of several City churches after the war gave opportunity to talented artists whose work in glass remains relatively unknown.

In compiling these walks I have tried to link together good examples of stained glass within particular parts of London. Routes have been chosen to take the reader through interesting streets, avoiding crowds and traffic as far as possible. Every walk begins and ends at an Underground station. Opening times and entry charges have been given as of August 2001.

Caroline Swash

Medieval stained glass 1250 - 1450

The six panels in the **Westminster Abbey Museum** are all that remain of the Norman scheme of decoration which must once have filled the windows, similar in subject and style (detail of St Nicholas panel) to continental work. Examples of glass contemporary with these  exquisite pieces can be seen in the **Victoria and Albert Museum** and in the **Queen's Chapel of the Savoy**.

Medieval glass can be found in Walks 1, 5, 8

Renaissance stained glass 1450 - 1714

The most impressive example of a **Renaissance** window in the Continental European manner can be seen at **St Margaret's Westminster**: purchased for the church in 1759.

Figurative and heraldic work like this example can be seen by the Dutch artists

Bernard and **Abraham van Linge** and the Englishman **Richard Butler** at **Lincoln's Inn Chapel.**

At **St George's,** Hanover Square there is a fine east

window, originally created by **Arnold of Nijmegen** for a Carmelite Church in Antwerp around 1520 and brought to London following the suppression of the enclosed religious orders by Napoleon.

At **St Katherine Cree** the rose window contains original glass from 1628 - 31 when the church was rebuilt. In **Sir John Soane's Museum** and the **Victoria and Albert Museum** panels and fragments of interesting painted glass from this period are on display.

Renaissance glass can be found in Walks 2, 5, 8, 12

Georgian stained glass
1714 -1815

At **Westminster Abbey** there are two fine examples of the work of **Sir James Thornhill**, sergeant painter to King George 1, who was commissioned to paint canvases for interpretation into glass. The north transept rose window was fabricated in 1721 by **Joshua Price** and the west window by his son **William Price** in 1733. A magnificent window made by James Pearson in 1788 can be seen in St Botolph Aldersgate and two roundels made in 1796 in St Mary's Battersea. During this period the fabricating artist worked from a painting using enamels as well as coloured glass to make the stained glass copy as close to the original as possible.

Georgian glass can be seen on Walk 1

Gothic Revival stained glass 1815 - 1860

Interest in Gothic art and architecture started as the romantic hobby of a few antiquarians and gradually grew into the popular architectural and decorative language that we know today as 'Victorian'. **Thomas Willement** was one of the first stained glass artists to be interested in this study. He was artist in stained glass to Queen Victoria and responsible for the renovation in 1839 - 42 of **Temple Church** in the new Gothic manner. Only six small scenes remain of this scheme. At **St Botolph, Aldgate** the east window by **Charles Clutterbuck** combines the Georgian practise of working from a painting (Rubens' Deposition) with the new interest in Medieval glass.

Gothic Revival glass can be seen on Walks 8, 12

Victorian stained glass 1860 onwards

The 1851 Great Exhibition and the construction between 1839 and 1860 of the new Houses of Parliament gave enormous impetus to the adoption of Gothic as the language of English and later Imperial Christendom. Church restoration and building in the new style was carried on with enthusiasm until the outbreak of the First World War in 1914.

The fabrication of a window during these hectic years usually took place in factory conditions with different craft skills (cutting, painting, firing, glazing) in the hands of a number of people. The architects involved in church commissions tended to employ their own stained glass firms. **Sir George Gilbert Scott** who worked on **Westminster Abbey, St Michael Cornhill** and the new church of **St Mary Abbots** gave the work of deco-

rating the interior as well as the stained
glass to two talented trainees **John
Clayton** and **Alfred Bell**. A detail of their
work from the gallery of **St John's
Church, Hampstead** is pictured here.
The firm, **Clayton and Bell**, became one
of the most successful and productive
during this time. Successive firms were
either trained by them - **John Burlison**
and **Thomas Grylls** for example - or

were rivals. The most active of these was **James Powell and Sons (Powells)** who later traded under the name of **Whitefriars**. Their glass can be seen in **St Edmund, King and Martyr**, **St John's Hampstead** and **St Botolph, Bishopsgate**.

However, **William Butterfield** the architect of **All Saints**, **Margaret Street** demanded precise conformity to his decorative plans and used individual craftsmen in preference to firms.

Many Victorian churches were built without stained glass. Clear glass in diamond shapes would be put into the window spaces, to be taken out and replaced with individual memorials. Fascinating examples of the evolution of taste and skill in windows of this kind can be seen at **St Barnabas, Addison Road**.

Victorian Glass can be seen in Walks 1, 2, 3, 4, 5, 11, 13

William Morris
& his contemporaries
1860 onwards

Although imbued with the love of the past, **William Morris** loathed the tidying up of medieval buildings carried out in the name of restoration and he refused to allow his firm to be involved in any of these projects. Designs for new stained glass windows were drawn up by his

friend, the visionary artist **Sir Edward Burne-Jones**. This 'Angeli Ministrates' can be seen at St Peter's, Vere Street. Many of his designs and cartoons, were used again and again over the years, long after both men were dead. Interesting windows by the firm can be seen at **St Peter's Vere Street, St Barnabas, Addison Road** and **Holy Trinity, Sloane Street**.

The **Aesthetic Movement** which developed alongside Morris' vision influenced the thoughtful neoclassical painter **Henry Holiday**. He made a superb west window for **Southwark Cathedral** and fine glass for **Westminster Abbey** and **St Margaret's Westminster**. His contemporary, the American artist **John La Farge** is also represented in the Cathedral with a fine window for the **Harvard Chapel**.

Work from William Morris & his contemporaries can be seen on Walks 1, 2, 3, 5, 13

The Arts & Crafts movement 1890 onwards

The attraction of Morris' ideas about the importance of the making of things, and the beauty of a life lived for art revolutionised attitudes amongst artists towards stained glass. **Christopher Whall**, the prime mover during this period, taught himself and then his students an awareness of the artistic possibilities within all aspects of fabrication.

The result was a personal response to the medium both refreshing and inspiring. Fine windows by Whall can be seen at **Holy Trinity, Sloane Street** and **Gray's Inn Chapel**. His followers, many of them women, created windows in the **University Church of Christ the King (Lilian Pocock)**, **St John's Hampstead (Joan Fulleylove)** and **St Etheldreda's Ely Place (J. Edward Nuttgens)**. John Byam Shaw who founded the Art School that bears his name created a fine window in this tradition at **St Barnabas, Addison Road**.

Although she was working from the 1930s onwards, **Evie Hone** should be included here. Her windows, like this example in the **Jesuit Church, Farm Street** and **St Michael's, Highgate** were designed and made with minimal assistance. Her training began as a Cubist in France and continued in glass in Ireland.

Glass from the Arts & Crafts movement can be seen on Walks 4 ,7, 14

Postwar Reconstruction 1945 - 65

The bombing of London during the Second World War destroyed most of the glass in the City. Restoration was entrusted to some remarkable architects who were enthusiastic about Sir Christopher Wren's buildings but alert to changes in church use.

The architects **Lord Mottistone and Paul Paget (Seely and Paget), Stephen Dykes Bower** and **W Godfrey Allen** all commissioned the artist **Brian Thomas** to make windows for the churches they restored. His glass can be seen in **St Paul's Cathedral, St Vedast, St Andrew's, Holborn** and **Westminster Abbey**. John Hayward worked for the firm **Faithcraft** which was involved in making furnishings as well as stained glass. His work can be seen at **St Mary-Le-Bow** and **St Michael, Paternoster Royal,** where this memorial to the benefactor of St Michaels, Lord Mayor of London, Dick Whittington and his cat may be seen.

Lawrence Lee, meanwhile, involved in building up the stained glass department of the Royal College of Art after the war, was also making new windows for **St Magnus Martyr, St Mary Aldermary** and later the **Museum of Garden History**.

Competitions resulted in the production of several interesting commissions. **Carl Edwards** made an east window for **Temple Church**. **Christopher Webb** created a fine illustrational Shakespeare memorial for **Southwark Cathedral**, as well as an entire scheme for **St Lawrence Jewry**.

Postwar glass can be seen on
Walks 1, 9, 10, 11, 12, 13

After Coventry
1965 - 1985

The impact of the radical new Coventry Cathedral by the architect Basil Spence was incalculable. Spence had used stained glass in an entirely new way giving opportunity to the artists **John Hutton, John Piper, Patrick Reyntiens** and **Margaret Traherne** as well as the Royal College team, **Lawrence Lee, Geoffrey Clarke** and **Keith New**. Suddenly stained glass seemed to be a dynamic new building material radiant with colour rather than a vehicle for church memorials.

Those involved in the Coventry project received new and interesting commissions. John Piper and Patrick Reyntiens made windows for **St Margaret's Westminster** and **Sanderson's Show Room** in Berners Street. **Keith New** made applique panels for the **Commonwealth Institute** and a Baptistery window for **All Hallows by the Tower**. The experimental approach suggested by Spence led to new windows being made with thick slab glass set in concrete (dalle de verre) and used as part of the building. Indeed, **Pierre Fourmaintraux** was invited from France by **Whitefriars** to work for the firm in this medium.

Post Coventry Cathedral
Glass may be seen on Walks
1, 2, 3, 5, 6, 12

The Contemporary scene

The immediate postwar years were influenced by French ideas concerning new uses of glass but after 1970 a shift in emphasis occurred largely due to influences emanating from **Swansea College of Art**. **Tim Lewis** who had been trained by Lawrence Lee at the Royal College became head of the glass department at Swansea in 1965 and initiated a series of visitor schemes to bring the most radical artists in Europe to Wales. He invited **Georg Meisterman, Ludwig Schaffrath** and **Johannes Schreiter** to lecture and build windows at the College. Many of the students at that time have become the most interesting designers of their day. These include **Alex Beleschenko, Amber Hiscott, Graham Jones** and **Martin Donlin**.

However, the most radical innovator during the 1980s and 1990s was **Brian**

Clarke. He too was inspired by the **Post War German School** and particularly fired by the example of Johannes Schreiter's life and work.

Recently artists have endeavoured to exploit the reliability of toughened sheet glass which can be obscured, textured and coloured in a variety of ways. Most of these commissions are for refurbishment schemes within offices, housing complexes, restaurants and bars.

Glass has also become a medium of interest in the world of fine art. Examples of new glass can be seen on a regular basis at the **London Glassblowing Workshop's Glass Art Gallery,** 7 The Leather Market, Weston Street near London Bridge and the **Cochrane Gallery** (above the Cochrane Theatre).

View contemporary glass on Walks 1, 3, 5, 6, 8, 12, 13

Walk 1
Around Westminster

 Start: Westminster
Finish: Pimlico

If you only have time for a few London
walks this is one you should do.
Westminster Abbey and **St Margaret's**
have fine examples of stained glass from
the Middle Ages to the present day giving
a wonderful overview of the development of the art.

 The Museum of Garden History
and **Tate Britain** both possess one window by a distinguished artist. However,
start early to avoid the crowds in
Westminster Abbey.

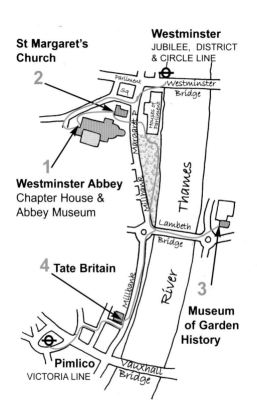

Westminster
JUBILEE, DISTRICT
& CIRCLE LINE

St Margaret's Church

2

Parliment Sq

Westminster Bridge

Margaret P

Houses of Parliment

Thames

1

Westminster Abbey
Chapter House &
Abbey Museum

Millbank

Lambeth Bridge

4 **Tate Britain**

Millbank

River

3

Museum of Garden History

Pimlico
VICTORIA LINE

Vauxhall Bridge

Walk 1

Around Westminster

1

Westminster Abbey
Open Mon - Sat 9.30 - 4.30
Admission charge
Sunday - Services only
**Chapter House
& Abbey Museum**
Open Mon - Sat 10.30 - 4.00
Cost £1.00 plus Abbey Ticket
Free to English Heritage

2

**St Margaret's Church
Westminster**
Open Mon - Sat 9.30 - 4.30
Sunday - Services only

3 **The Museum
of Garden History**
Lambeth Palace Road
Open from first Sun in Feb to
second Sun in Dec
Mon - Fri 10.30 - 5.00
Sun 10.30 - 5.00
Closed Sat
Admission charge

4 **Tate Britain**
Millbank
10.00 - 6.00
Open daily

Refreshments
Westminster Abbey
The Museum of Garden History
Tate Britain

walk 1

Westminster Abbey

The Abbey has a one way system starting from the north transept.

Enter and look across to

1   The south transept rose by **John Burlison** and **Thomas Grylls** completed in 1901 in time for King Edward VII's Coronation, replacing a Ward and Nixon window on the same theme 'The Preparation of the Ancient World for Christ' which the Dean and Chapter found too vivid. Orderly rows of figures placed under architectural canopies combined with the careful balance of colour give a sense of grandeur and dignity to this part of the building.

Follow the one way system into the Henry VII Chapel

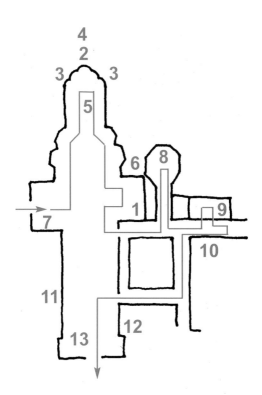

4
2
3   3
5
6   8
1   9
7
10
11
12
13

walk 1

2   The 'Battle of Britain' window (1946 - 49) by **Hugh Easton** is by far his best in the Abbey. The lively interpretation of the badges of the Royal Air Force Squadrons within an arboreal framework has been combined with 'Visions' representing different branches of the service. The figures of the airmen were drawn from one model, a young flight officer Hugh Martin Neil. Male seraphim above represent the heavenly host who are 'welcoming the fallen into Paradise'.

3   **Alfred Fisher** of **Chapel Studios** designed a series of shields for windows in the apsidal chapels commemorating those who contributed to the recent restoration of the Abbey. Lettering and symbol have been pleasantly combined.

4   In November 2000, **Alan Younger** completed an attractive blue and rose window for the clerestory at the east end of the Henry VII Chapel. Given by Lord and Lady Harris of Peckham, the pictorial elements cluster around the subject of the Virgin Mary.

Look towards the west end of the chapel

5   The completion of the restoration of the Abbey was commemorated by this fine window designed by **John Lawson** of **Goddard and Gibbs Studios** in conjunction with the Abbey architect **Donald Buttress**. Simple strongly drawn heraldic emblems have been enhanced with colour and stain and set within clear glass to form a most successful backdrop to the west end of the chapel.

6   This elegant painterly window was created by **Graham Jones** in 1994 to allow space for the commemoration of poets in **Poet's Corner**. Predominantly blue, enhanced by wreaths of coloured flowers, the background glass has been made pale to admit light through the upper sections of the window. Jones, pictured right, worked on this window himself in his studio at Kew with help from **John Reyntiens**.

7   The rose window was designed by **James Thornhill** in 1721 and made by **Joshua Price**. The subject was the 'Twelve Apostles' with cherubim around them and the open bible in the centre.   Between 1884 - 93 the architect **John L Pearson** repaired and rearranged the stonework and shortened and darkened the figures to make the window fashionably Gothic.

Following bomb damage, **Brian Thomas** added six windows below the rose in 1957 in a rich sombre baroque style. The subjects for each powerful window are the 'Acts of Mercy' to the hungry, thirsty, homeless, naked, sick and those in prison. The strongly coloured decorative frames to these monochrome scenes were inspired by ceiling decoration in this part of the Abbey.

Continue through the cloister to the Chapter House

8 Stained glass by **Clayton and Bell** was restored and rearranged by **Joan Howson** after bomb damage. She added poignant personal wartime details painted onto the background diamonds near the entrance. Note the mourning figure with the question: 'Why'?

Continue to the Abbey Museum

9 Six exquisite thirteenth century **Medieval** panels were superbly restored by **Chapel Studios** in 1986 and can now be examined in detail. Fragments like these had a profound influence on later artists searching for spiritual inpiration.

Pause to see

10   A delicate memorial window by **Francis Skeat** typical of the illustrational style popular during the 1950s.

Continue to the nave of the Abbey and look across to the north side

11   Here we can see the magnificent series of historical windows by **Ninian Comper** depicting kings and abbots, made between 1909 and 1962 (the last by his nephew **Arthur Bucknall**). The background has been enriched by illustrations of people and events relating to the life and work of the subject. Drawings painted onto glass were Comper's special skill, revealing his mastery of the figure and his breadth of learning, aspects of stained glass work

much admired by his followers and suc-
cessors **Christopher** and **Geoffrey Webb**,
Hugh Easton and **Francis Skeat**.

Look across to the south side

12   The memorial to **Isambard
Kingdom Brunel** is an early **Henry
Holiday** window made by **Heaton,
Butler** and **Bayne**, revealing Holiday's
admiration for the work of the Pre-
Raphaelites in the scale and colour of the
figure compositions, which deal with incidents in the building and rebuilding of the
'Temple at Jerusalem'; fit subject for an
engineer. The virtues of 'Fortitude,
Justice, Faith and Charity' have been represented in the classical manner by female
personification. Here Holiday's own
emerging style can be seen.

Look towards the west end

13 The great west window was designed by **Sir James Thornhill** and made by **William Price** in 1733. Thornhill was the King's painter and a designer of mural and ceiling decorations. Price's job was to copy the paintings of Patriarchs and Prophets commissioned for the scheme faithfully onto glass using paint and enamel to express the dramatic impact of each figure.

On leaving the Abbey turn right and follow the path to nearby St Margaret's.

St Margaret's Westminister

At the east end

This dark **Renaissance** window was bought for the Church in 1759. It is a 'Crucifixion' scene following continental models in composition and iconography. The 'Royal Portraits' on either side are thought to depict King Henry VIII and his first wife Catherine of Aragon with their Patron Saints, St George and St Catherine, above.

On the south side

An underestimated series of abstract windows 'Spring in London' were designed by **John Piper** and made by **Patrick Reyntiens** in 'gentle yellows, greens, whites and silver greys.' They should be viewed as a wall of glass interacting with and complementing the carved plaques and memorials set into this part of the building.

At the west end

Henry Holiday's fine window was commissioned to mourn the murder of Lord Frederick Cavendish. Here the figure of Christ is attended by women and grieving angels in anguished flight. Below there are scenes from the New Testament accompanied by inscriptions. In the traceries Holiday has placed elegant posturing angels.

Above the west door

Frederic W. Farrar, when rector of St Margaret's, used his American contacts to facilitate the commissioning of new glass during the nineteenth century. The 'Raleigh' window stresses the connection between Elizabethan England and the United States. Here, **Clayton and Bell** have given historical figures the status of saints in formal dress under fourteenth century style canopies.

Next to the Raleigh window

The 'John Milton' window, also by Clayton and Bell, shows the poet surrounded by illustrations of scenes taken from his two most famous poems 'Paradise Lost' and 'Paradise Regained'. The borders are particularly inventive here.

The north side

Following bomb damage, the stained glass was relocated in windows on the north side of the church. Most of the surviving glass was designed by **Edward Frampton** in a florid and expansive style. Note the strange 'Ashurst' window in which two brothers are reunited in a heavenly arbour. This win-

Edward Ashurst Morris erected by his brother

dow features a copy in glass of the painting 'The Mystical Nativity' by Botticelli, just acquired at that time for the newly founded National Gallery.

Cross to Houses of Parliament, bear right through gardens and cross Lambeth Bridge.

St Mary at Lambeth
The Museum of
Garden History

On the north side opposite the entrance

Lawrence Lee created an enchanting window in 1972 on the subject of the two botanical explorers (father and son) both called **John Tradescant**. This lively work successfully mixes gardening references

with scenes illustrating gardens including the oriental garden above.

The window reveals the artist's interest in exploring different ways of using glass paint. Here new effects have been achieved with the aid of sponges and cut cardboard as well as brushes of different thickness. Lee was a hugely influential teacher at the Royal College of Art during the 1950s and 1960s, training Tim Lewis, Keith New and Geoffrey Clarke, Jane Gray and Ray Bradley. Within his studio he taught many assistants, among them Alan Younger.

In the Lady Chapel

Francis Stephens designed the remaining stained glass. Look for his attractive small window of the pedlar and his dog.

Go back over Lambeth Bridge and turn left along Millbank.

Walk 1

Tate Britain

The window is near the main entrance above the stairs leading to the cafe

One of the many Jewish refugees who came to England during the 1930s was the lively and gifted Hungarian artist **Ervin Bossanyi**. This window was created for Tate Britain under incredibly difficult circumstances between 1937 and 1948. Its subject grew from a moment experienced by the artist during a visit to Chartres Cathedral.

'One morning I watched the washerwomen in the valley as they were busily washing, rinsing, wringing and shaking the clothes. What a wonderful work they achieve, I thought and yet there is in the cathedral not one window for them. But I will make one for them....and as I looked up to see the spires of the church, it seemed to me

that the angel descends......and brings
purification and a heavenly benediction'.

*Leave through the main door, turn right and
right again up Atterbury Street, left at John
Islip then right to cross Vauxhall Bridge Road.
Continue on Drummond Gate and Bessborough
Street to Pimlico Underground.*

Walk 2
Around Oxford Circus

Start: Bond Street
Finish: Tottenham Court Road

St Peter's, Vere Street contains several fine windows by **Edward Burne-Jones** for **Morris and Co** including the superb 'Christ's Entry into Jerusalem'. Interesting windows by **Powells** have been added to match. **All Saints, Margaret Street** is one of the really great churches of Victorian England, and its architect **William Butterfield** took enormous care to commission fitting stained glass. An exotic wall of coloured glass by **John Piper** and **Patrick Reyntiens** can be seen at the **Sanderson Hotel**.

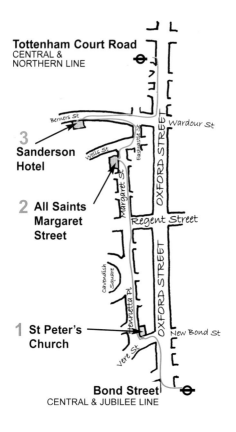

Tottenham Court Road
CENTRAL &
NORTHERN LINE

Berners St

Wardour St

3

**Sanderson
Hotel**

Wells St

Eastcastle St

OXFORD STREET

2 **All Saints
Margaret
Street**

Margaret St

Regent Street

Cavendish
Square

OXFORD STREET

Henrietta Pl

1 **St Peter's
Church**

New Bond St

Vere St

Bond Street
CENTRAL & JUBILEE LINE

Walk 2

Around Oxford Circus

1

St Peter's Church
Vere Street
Open Mon - Fri 9.00 - 5.00
Closed Sat - Sun

2

All Saints Church
Margaret Street
Open Daily 7.00 - 7.00

3

Sanderson Hotel
50 Berners Street
The restaurant at this Ian
Schrager Hotel is open to
non-residents from 7.30 am

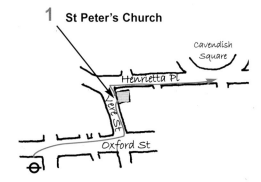

1 St Peter's Church

Cavendish
Square

Henrietta Pl

Vere St

Oxford St

Bond Street
CENTRAL LINE

Refreshments

Available all along the route

Walk

St Peter's Vere Street

The Institute for Contemporary Christianity

East end

This window was designed to light a painting by **Edward Burne-Jones** entitled 'The Morning of the Resurrection' which showed Mary Magdalene meeting Jesus outside the tomb with angels in attendance. This painting was given to the church in memory of the Christian Socialist, F Denison Maurice, Vicar of St Peters from 1860 - 69. The painting was sold during the 1980s to pay for the reordering of the Church. However, a version of the same subject is in the possession of **Tate Britain**.

The window's subject was linked to the painting. Here Christ offers the woman of Samaria the 'Water of Life'. As in the painting, angels attend the central scene. Burne-Jones' passion for the work of early Renaissance artists can be seen in the clothing and posture of the figures.

On the south side

Here we have a wonderful view of **Burne-Jones'** 'Christs Entry into Jerusalem' for which he made a coloured cartoon. He was paid £85 by the firm, a sum that he described as a 'mean total'. Again Italian influences can be seen. The rocky landscape and stubby trees, robed apostles and palm bearing followers in clear bright colours recall compositions by Botticelli and Giotto.

The design for 'Angeli Ministrantes' was made by **Burne-Jones** for stained glass windows in Salisbury Cathedral. Two angels pause on their journey along life's path. Each carries a staff, food and drink. Magnificent wings frame their romantic faces and they stand within one of **William Morris**' favourite acanthus leaf decorative surrounds. The photograph shows the friends in old age, Morris is seated.

A fine window by **Powells** was made to match those designed by **Burne-Jones**. The figures are similar in size and set within a foliate border. 'Faith and Hope' have been personified as girls and given appro-  priate symbols. Hope's flowering branch has been particularly well observed and painted.

Turn right when leaving the church, proceed down Henrietta Place, crossing Regent Street and continue down Margaret Street. All Saints will be on your left.

All Saints, Margaret St

This is a superb complete church (1849 - 59) by the architect **William Butterfield** who personally supervised the stained glass in order to create a highly decorative unified sacred interior.

South windows

Both windows are by **Alexander Gibbs**. The subjects consist of three archangels Raphael, Michael and Gabriel, detail left, and and two figures representing the Eastern and Western church, St Athanasius and St Augustine of Hippo. Here in more brilliant form are the olive greens, brick reds, mauves and whites of the wall tiles ordered into a composition both patterned yet recognisably figurative.

This 'Tree of Jesse' is the second to be installed. Butterfield's intention was to have a copy of the great C14 'Jesse Tree' window in Wells Cathedral made for his west window.

However, he disliked the first version by the French artist **Alfred Gérente** complaining that the green glass had a 'cabbage' quality. Removing this window after the dedication of the church, he ordered a better copy from **Alexander Gibbs**.

It is interesting to compare the iconography. For example the robust C14 depiction of Christ suckling at his mothers' breast has been tidied up for All Saints. Here the child sits sideways on his mothers knee holding her hand. The gesture is comforting but lacks the force of the earlier version.

Sanderson Hotel

John Piper created this imaginative wall
of glass in 1959. Here plant forms have
been enlarged to make a lively and
unusual background for visitors ascend-
ing the stairs to Sanderson's fabric
showroom. The confident simplified
shapes and unusual juxtapositions of
colour reveal Piper's enthusiasm for the
work of Matisse as well as his own love
of plants and gardens - which he

explored so often
in paint and print.
Patrick Reyntiens
who interpreted
the designs into
glass managed to
bring variety of
surface and colour
to these curious
organic forms.

3 Sanderson Hotel

Berners St

Tottenham Court Road
CENTRAL &
NORTHERN LINE

East Castle St

Oxford St

2 All Saints Margaret St

Walk 2

Walk 3

Around Kensington

 Start & Finish
High Street Kensington

10 minute walk to Leighton House or
hop on a bus to Melbury Road

Leighton House and **Linley Sambourne House** have both been preserved with care and contain stained glass as an important part of the decorative effect. **St Barnabas Church** possesses a sequence of windows which reveal the development of the **Gothic Revival** and a rare **Arts and Crafts** window by **John Byam Shaw**. **St Mary Abbots** has a complete scheme of stained glass and furnishings by **Clayton and Bell**. Modern glass can be seen at **The Commonwealth Institute (Keith New)** and at **Leighton House (Ray Bradley)**.

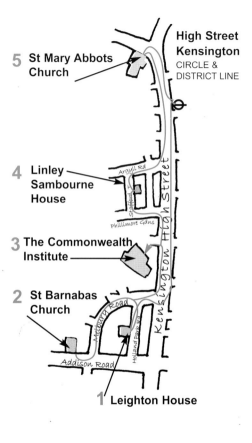

High Street Kensington
CIRCLE & DISTRICT LINE

5 St Mary Abbots Church

4 Linley Sambourne House

Argyll Rd

Stafford T

Phillimore Gdns

3 The Commonwealth Institute

2 St Barnabas Church

Melbury Road

Kensington Hign Street

Holland Park Rd

Addison Road

1 Leighton House

Walk 3

Around Kensington

1

Leighton House
Holland Park Road
Open 11.00 - 5.30
Closed Tues

2

St Barnabas Church
Addison Road
Open by arrangement
stbk.org.uk
Tel: (020) 7471-7000
Fax: (020) 7471-7001

3 **The Commonwealth Institute**
Kensington High Street
Open by arrangement
Tel: (020) 7603-4535
Ask for conference office

4 **Linley Sambourne House**
Stafford Terrace
Guided Tours (Sat. & Sun.)
Call (0207) 602 3316
for information.
Admission charge

5 **St Mary Abbots Church**
Church Street
Open Daily 7.00 - 7.00

Refreshments
Along Kensington High Street

Leighton House

On the ground floor of the artist, **Lord Leighton's**, house there are 8 windows from Damascus set into the dome of the sumptuous **Arab Hall** with its tiled walls and fountain. These windows made of glass and plaster were restored and regilded in 1987 by **David Wasley**. One of the elegant inscriptions reads 'dry food for livestock'. Upstairs a single similar window designed by the architect **George Aitchison** divides the summer and winter studios. Here we can see the techniques used, the angled openings and the sculptural effect of the plaster.

The living rooms and studio contain paintings by Leighton and his contemporaries, including the cartoon drawing by Burne-Jones for one of the windows in the Morris room in the Victoria and Albert Museum.

To separate the winter studio from the **Upper Perrin Gallery**, Ray Bradley has created superb screen printed glass doors (1995). Based on the pattern made by the wicker screens in the Arab Hall, the positive/negative shapes have been angled so that they alternate and shift according to the movement of the viewer.

2 St Barnabas Church
1 Leighton House
3 Commonwealth Institute

Melbury Road
Addison Road
Holland Park Rd
Kensington High Street

St Barnabas Church

Near the door there are two fine windows made in 1902 by the artist and teacher **John Byam Shaw** (1872-1919) who was a lifelong member of the congregation. Shaw founded the Byam Shaw School of Art which continues to flourish to this day. Evie Hone was a student of his and he was one of the first to recognise her talent.

'St Cecilia' and 'St Margaret' are typical of the period. Both are represented as

 young girls and perhaps drawn from the same model. The coloured glass has been carefully selected and painted (almost certainly by Shaw himself) in the Arts and Crafts tradition.

North side

On the wall look for Byam Shaw's memorial plaque which he made himself: an enchanting picture in the Flemish style of St Luke painting the Virgin Mary within a turreted wooden frame decorated with stencilled patterns.

South side

In the clerestory windows, stained glass was installed between 1850 and 1900. The windows were added as funds permitted and made by different firms, thus revealing the gradual development of Victorian taste from quite primitive imitations of Medieval windows 'Christ the Good Shepherd' with his doggy sheep to sumptuous pictorial compositions 'Martha and Mary' in which biblical scenes and characters have been presented in a style combining a sense of luxury with an educational interest in medieval costume and surroundings.

West end

The superb west window by **Michael O'Connor** was commissioned for the east window in 1851. The subject 'Christ and the Twelve Apostles' has been arranged as a frieze with Christ in the centre and three of the twelve on either side. The other six, who are all looking up, would have occupied the lower row in the original setting. The figures show a thoughtful approach to characterisation, while considerable care has been taken with the arrangement of gestures and robes to create balanced blocks of colour. This is an example of Gothic Revival glass at its best.

The chancel

The **Clayton and Bell** window which
replaced O'Connor's east window glass
shows the effect of mass production on
the standards of this once interesting firm.

Here there are two windows by **Morris
and Co** using cartoons made by **Edward
Burne-Jones** for other churches. 'Miriam
and Ruth' were originally drawn in 1886
for St Giles Cathedral, Edinburgh, while
the 'Angels Carrying Palms and Musical
Instruments' were both designed in 1874
for Christ Church Oxford. The
'Trumpet Blowing Angels' opposite were
designed in 1869 for St Edward the
Confessor's church in Chedleton,
Staffordshire. Considerable liberties were
often taken by the firm for financial rea-
sons since a background of clear glass
was cheaper to make than a landscape or
foliate pattern.

The Commonwealth Institute

In the Entrance Foyer there are a series
of panels by **Keith New** made in 1960 in
which layers of carefully arranged
coloured glass have been glued onto
sheets of clear float glass to provide a
visually exciting background to photographs of Commonwealth personalities.
Appliqué glass - as this technique was
called - derived from the desire to use
glass for the sake of colour without any
'churchy' connotations. However, since
many of the bonding materials were
unstable and the buildings liable to
change of use, few examples of this technique have survived.

Go back to Kensington High Street, turning left.
Take another left on Phillimore Gardens, then
right onto Stafford Terrace. The house is half
way up on your right.

Linley Sambourne House

Edward Linley Sambourne (1844-1910) and his wife Marion moved to 18 Stafford Terrace in 1874 just after their

marriage. Their house was built as part of the development of the west of London beyond the newly built cultural centres of the South Kensington Museums and the Albert Hall. Linley Sambourne worked as a cartoonist for Punch and seems to have been a lively character with a wonderful sense of humour. Shortly after the couple moved in they entirely refurbished the house in what was then the modern Aesthetic style, probably much influenced by Sambourne's circle of artistic friends, some of whom lived nearby. This refurbishment included several stained glass windows.

The morning room

The coloured glass in all the windows accorded with Aesthetic ideas about the toning of light. Heraldry was still popular, linking in imagination the town dwelling home owner with the baron in his hall. Sambourne commissioned family shields to hang in a row suspended on a metal rod. The pattern for the diapers below consist of alternating flowers and suns.

Garden door

Just as typical of this period is the glass door panel leading out to the small square garden. This is an exceptionally attractive version of a fruiting, flowering peach tree; symbol of good fortune. The container is a bowl patterned with ducks, frogs and fish. Daffodils, sunflowers, daisies and foxgloves support the base and a charming pattern of dog roses and leaves form a frame.

Upstairs landing

Going upstairs, this family monogram can be seen inter- twined and set within a multi- coloured boss embellished with roses.

Drawing room

This is the most splendid window of all.
According to a journalist on the Pall Mall
Gazette writing in 1889, Linley
Sambourne himself designed this window:

'My own design ..... there is the rising
sun, and birds on the wing, something to
make London more cheerful.' Unusual
elements in this window are the parrot
and crow, and the palm branches. The
branches make an exotic frame for the
central decoration of quarries containing
the family references: the Sambourne star
and Herapath lion.

St Mary Abbots Church

A late splendid church by the architect **George Gilbert Scott** with furnishings and glass by **Clayton and Bell**. Looking eastward, the vista rises layer by layer crowned by the five-light east window, a perfect and complete ensemble.

North transept

These windows by Clayton and Bell were added in 1877 and 1878. Here the architectural canopy has disappeared and the scenes have been stacked on top of each other, divided by horizontal bands.

'Twelve Parables' fill one four-light window, 'Twelve Miracles' the other. All the little incidental things, the plants, birds and bits of drapery, have received the kind of attention that makes detail a pleasure to look at.

South transept

Here all the windows illustrate 'The Life of St Paul': a remarkable achievement in such a small space. The saint himself can be identified by his dome shaped head though not by his clothes which alter as the story progresses. The tale begins at the bottom of the left hand light with a scene showing Saul being presented with the Roman authorization to persecute Christians, and continues through several episodes to end at the top of the far right hand lancet in which Paul tells the Jews why he has come to Rome. The disentangling of the various goings on must have kept many a baffled child quiet during the long sermons which were part of a Victorian morning service.

West window

It is fascinating to compare this window with the east window at the other end. Here at a glance, can be seen the enormous extent to which the Aesthetic Movement in art and fashion had influenced the feelings and perceptions of designers and their clients. Patriarchs and

prophets have been chosen as appropriate subjects and placed, richly costumed, against a grisaille background under little groves of trees which give them a strangely pastoral air. The scenes placed below each figure illustrate a relevant event.

The colour is entirely different. Gone are the sharp alternations of red, blue and white to be replaced by an autumnal impression conveyed by golds and greens. That Clayton and Bell's espousal of this altered viewpoint was not entirely successful is hardly surprising. Both were convinced Gothic Revivalists and their handling of a different, more emotional, approach seems uneasy. The figures have a slightly bombastic air, as if straining for theatrical effect.

Aisles and clerestory

Here the sheer scale of the building in its original state becomes apparent. In spite of the removal of the background, the remaining glass can be appreciated as a series of pictures of which no two are the same. Within the limited range of an archaic style, their inventiveness is quite remarkable and it is worth wandering round to see them all. With an effort it is possible to imagine how dark and glimmering, how otherwordly and strangely romantic this whole interior must have been, before the canopies and borders were taken out and light glass put in. Fortunately the poet John Betjeman's enthusiasm for Victorian architecture  expressed in articles and interviews during the 1960s helped to prevent further destruction of the stained glass of this period.

Walk 4

Around Mayfair

Start: Green Park *exit*
Piccadilly North Side
Finish: Oxford Circus

A long interesting walk through
Georgian and **Victorian** London. **Evie
Hone's** windows for **The Church of
the Immaculate Conception** show this
great colourist at her best. While at **St
George's Hanover Square** there is a
fine early **Renaissance** window by the
Flemish artist **Arnold of Nijmegen**.
Original glass and an **Art Nouveau** win-
dow can be seen at **Thomas Goode &
Co**. The new canopy for the Taisei com-
pany on Hanover Street by **Kate Maestri**
is easy to find. After a detour through
Liberty & Co, an example of **Martin
Donlin's** work can be seen nearby.

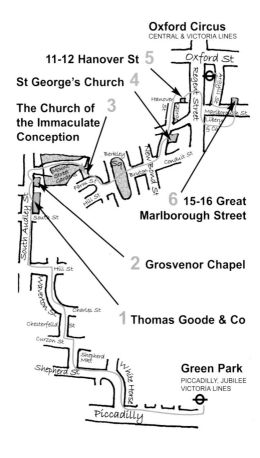

Oxford Circus
CENTRAL & VICTORIA LINES

Oxford St

11-12 Hanover St 5

St George's Church 4

The Church of the Immaculate Conception 3

Regent Street

Hanover St

George St

Argyll St

Marlborough St

Liberty & Co

Berkley Sq

New Bond St

Conduit St

Mount Street Gardens

Farm St

Bruton St

Hill St

6 **15-16 Great Marlborough Street**

South Audley St

South St

2 **Grosvenor Chapel**

Hill St

Waverton St

Charles St

Chesterfeild St

1 **Thomas Goode & Co**

Curzon St

Shepherd Mkt

Shepherd St

White Horse

Green Park
PICCADILLY, JUBILEE VICTORIA LINES

Piccadilly

Walk 4

Around Mayfair

1 **Thomas Goode & Co**
South Audley Street
Open Mon - Sat 9.30 - 5.00

2 **Grosvenor Chapel**
South Audley Street
Open Mon - Fri 9.30 - 1.00
Concerts Tues 1.10
Sunday - Services only

3 **The Church of the Immaculate Conception**
Farm Street
Open Daily 7.00 - 7.00

4 **St George's Church**
Hanover Square
Open Mon - Fri 10.00 - 3.00
Sunday - Services only

5 **11 - 12 Hanover Street**
Exterior view only

6 **15 - 16 Great
Marlborough Street**
Exterior & reception only

Refreshments

Liberty & Co. and round Piccadilly
and Shepherd Market

4 walk

Thomas Goode & Co

The shop was built in the 1870's by the architects **Ernest George and Peto** in the newly fashionable red brick Queen Anne style. Exterior features include sunflower railings and roundels containing - among other things - a portrait of the family dog.

At the back of the shop, there is a stained glass window originally made for **Mr Goode's office**. This shows an idyllic outdoor scene set in a vaguely classical world in which practical tasks are performed by young girls in slightly seductive ways. A wall with fruit trees and peacocks provide the background.

Elsewhere in this fascinating emporium, there is a rare **Art Nouveau** window showing two girls reclining on the ground, one painting and the other writing with a landscape beyond and flowers in the foreground. Most of the composition has been cut from carefully selected coloured opalescent glass typical of the period.

Almost next door

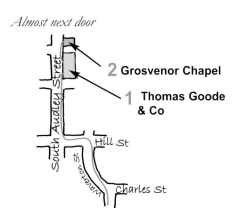

2 **Grosvenor Chapel**

1 **Thomas Goode & Co**

South Audley Street

Hill St

Mount St

Charles St

4
walk

Grosvenor Chapel

In 1913 **Ninian Comper** altered the east end
adding the rood screen with figures and
stained glass for the windows on the south
side. These elegant linear windows made in
clear bright colours, warm the interior in an

unobtrusive way. Look for Comper's personal mark: a wild strawberry.

Exit Grosvenor Chapel, turn right, then right again to walk straight ahead through St George's Gardens. Enter the church through the small door off the garden.

The Church of the Immaculate Conception

This church was built for the **Jesuits** in the 1840s by **J J Scoles** in a grand fourteenth century Gothic style.

The east window

This is a Tree of Jesse window by the Catholic firm **John Hardman** of Birmingham, rich, dark and fanciful.

The west rose

Following war damage, the west end was remodelled by **Adrian Gilbert Scott**, son of George Gilbert Scott. When it was finished, the great Irish artist **Evie Hone** was invited to make new stained glass for the rose. The subjects selected were the '41 Emblems of the Passion'. Here the chalice and patten of the 'Last

Supper', the nails, spear, whip and ladder of the 'Crucifixion', St Peter's cockerel and St Veronica's veil and other signs and symbols have been set out with almost childlike simplicity against backgrounds of intense red and blue glass. Arranged in this way, the geometry of the window has been enhanced and each of the many traceries filled with coherent images and satisfying colour.

Years of study in France under the cubist painter Albert Gleizes had given Hone considerable understanding of the control of colour and shape which she used to such good effect in glass.

Hone's affection for early celtic stone carving can be seen in the two figures set into the wall above the Rose. 'St Mary and St Joseph' are perfect in their own terms, both new yet somehow ancient.

The 'Assumption of Christ's Mother into Heaven' is the subject of this window made by **Evie Hone** in 1953. Here, Mary, a peasant girl, rises above her tomb watched by equally humble attendants. The colour is earthy and the emotional impact brooding. Hone's debt to the French painter Rouault is evident here in the painting of the faces and hands. The

completion of these windows towards the end of her life was a remarkable achievement. An early victim of polio, Hone struggled continually with physical disability which she overcame in the most admirable way producing an astonishing body of original work in glass and paint.

The third set of windows at the west end were made by **Patrick Pollen** in 1964 - working from the studio that Hone used in Dublin - The Glass Tower. Hone had already submitted a design to the church on the subject of St Ignatius but died (in 1955) before the window was commissioned. Pollen based these windows on her drawings, adapting his own style in order to match hers and give a sense of unity to the west end.

Exit the west end of the church, left along Farm Street, left at Hill Street, continue across Berkeley Square to Bruton Street. Cross Bond Street and go up Conduit Street, take the first left up St George's Street. St Georges Church is on your right.

4
walk

St George's Church

Here there is an amazing Renaissance east window, a 'Tree of Jesse' made by **Arnold of Nijmegen** for the three light east window of the Church of the Carmelite Nuns in Antwerp.

Sold by order of Napoleon, the glass was bought for St George's in 1840 and fitted into the church's much smaller windows by the Victorian stained glass artist **Thomas Willement.** He rearranged

the window, excising God from the top and the feet of Jesse and the Patriarchs at the base. He placed some of the ancestors of Christ into the flanking windows and added roundels of his own in imitation of those decorating the richly ornamental throne.

Arnold of Nijmegen was highly regarded in his day for his skill as a glass painter. The charm of his work can best be seen in his interpretation of the Virgin, an exquisite doll like girl poised elegantly on the moon with her baby in her arms.

A window by **F C Eden** (who sheltered Bossanyi during the war years) can be seen in the chapel.

Turn right up St George St to Hanover Square, turn right on Hanover St, 11-12 is on the right.

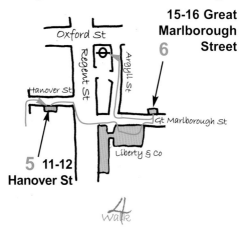

11 - 12 Hanover Street

One of the requirements for planning consent was the inclusion of public art in the building. **Kate Maestri** was approached by architects **DEGW** to provide an attractive canopy to the entrance of their office development for clients Taisei. Here Maestri has created a delicate striped awning in blues and greens to give a light contemporary feel to the red brick facade

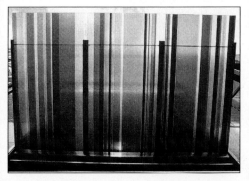

of this speculative office development. Her inspiration grew from a sense of the suitability of natural references (sky and trees) in this busy part of London.

Maestri was trained at Chelsea in Public Art and at Central Saint Martins where she studied glass. She is one of an increasing band of young designers using the technique of screen printing on safety glass to create new effects in light and colour.

For this commission, the technical process of screen printing was carried out by **David Proto** at his Glasshouse Fields studio in London.

4
walk

On the way to see Martin Donlin's glass, go into Liberty and Co at the Kirby Street entrance and bear right to find the main staircase of the original shop. Go up the stairs admiring the fragments of early glass which have been leaded into the windows. On the third floor, William Morris fabrics and tapestries designed by Burne-Jones can still be purchased. Leave the shop by the Marlborough Street exit and look out for the original doorway which features the thick 'norman slab' glass so often used by Arts and Crafts artists.

15 -16 Great Marlborough Street

Once the technology existed for the fabrication of large sheets of toughened glass, glazed entrances became popular in London. In 1999, **Martin Donlin** was invited to enhance these doorways with a lively design exploiting the contrasting textures on the  surface of the glass itself. He also used lenses to bring sparkle to this recessed space, picking up the glitter of the unusual twisted metal door handles. The pavement area has been ornamented with inset carved lettering - cryptic statements - which help to locate the entrances within the street.

Walk 5

Around Chelsea

1 French Institute
Queensberry Place
Open Tues - Fri 10.00 - 6.00
Library - Tues - Fri 12.00 -
6.00
Sat 12.00 - 7.00
Closed Monday

2 Church of Jesus Christ & Latter Day Saints
Exhibition Road
Open Mon - Fri 10.00 - 5.00
Closed Sat - Sun

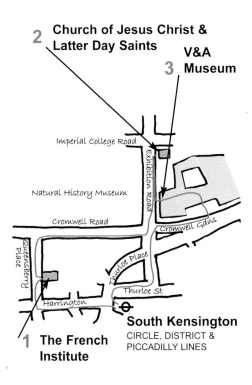

2 Church of Jesus Christ &
Latter Day Saints

3 V&A
Museum

Imperial College Road

Exhibition Road

Natural History Museum

Cromwell Road

Cromwell Gdns

Queensberry Place

Thurloe Place

Thurloe St

South Kensington
CIRCLE, DISTRICT &
PICCADILLY LINES

Harrington

1 The French
Institute

Walk 5

Around Chelsea

1

French Institute
Queensberry Place
Open Tues - Fri 10.00 - 6.00
Library - Tues - Fri 12.00 -
6.00
Sat 12.00 - 7.00
Closed Monday

2

**Church of Jesus Christ
& Latter Day Saints**
Exhibition Road
Open Mon - Fri 10.00 - 5.00
Closed Sat - Sun

3 Victoria and Albert Museum

Open Daily 10.00 - 5.45
Children free

Refreshments

French Institute
V & A. Museum
Many cafes in nearby streets

The French Institute

The 1939 Institute by architect **Patrice Bonnet** is a highly original building. Inspired use of brickwork has been enhanced by his unusual selection of

glass. Special tints were ordered for the windows of the **Grand Salon** - now the **Library**.

Outside the colour appears mauve against the white window tiles, inside the light is coloured pink. For the grand staircase Bonnet set blocks of clear glass in a concrete grid which counterpoints the elegant sweep of the steps.

Church of Jesus Christ & Latter Day Saints

The tower with **slab glass** inclusion has two main functions. It serves to display the religious nature of the building from the outside while bringing colour into the stairwell which it helps to conceal.

The coloured glass was designed by **Pierre Fourmaintraux** for **Whitefriars**.

The technique used in fabrication involved placing faceted blocks of glass into a frame, pouring in cement and allowing the block to set, thus creating a solid and colourful building material.

This system was perfected in France during the 1950s as a way of updating the visual language of Medieval windows and was brought to England by Fourmaintraux at the invitation of Whitefriars.

Here the external elevation reveals the pattern of glass within the cement forming gentle interlocking upward movements. Inside the effect is dramatic. The bright colours isolated within the concrete make daylight vivid and at night provide a glittering reminder of the church's presence.

Enter the V&A through the Henry Cole entrance on Exhibition Road.

Victoria and Albert Museum

Start at Henry Cole Wing.

Staircase windows

'From Icarus to Alex' is an early work by **Amber Hiscott** using glass for its surface qualities, its glitter or opacity.

The lead line in this panel has been used to draw the shape of the winged creature and hint at its destruction.

'Paddle Your own Canoe' was made during the winter of 1975-76 by **Richard Posner.** This panel incorporates all kinds of new techniques including the revived copper foil method of binding glass together. This is a fine example of  the pioneering work being done in California at this time.

'Brittany Beach' by **John Piper** and **Patrick Reyntiens** has many of the qualities associated with Piper's enormous output in paint and print. There is a romantic sense of place and time: a seascape with the tide out, an upturned boat, a house in the distance, all interpreted by Reyntiens in glass with tact and verve.

This backlit panel is by one of the most influential German designers **Ludwig Schaffrath**. It is a replica of one of six windows made in 1976 for the Hospital Chapel in Eschweiler, Germany.

Completely unpainted, the composition, suggesting hands or flames or birds, has been presented in an entirely linear way. Indeed Schaffrath's rhythmic use of different lead widths and his predilection for textured and opalescent white glass had considerable impact on ideas for architectural use from the 1980s onwards.

Take the lift to the Frank Lloyd Wright Gallery

Frank Lloyd Wright's famous window 'Kindersymphony' (1912) can be seen here along with furnishings and pho-

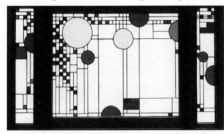

tographs of his buildings. The abstract shapes, circles, squares and flags in the window were intended to suggest a passing parade for the children in the Cooney Playhouse at Riverside, Illinois.

Continue by lift to the Ionides Collection

A rare opportunity to see a collection of popular paintings by Victorian artists as well as early decorated furniture, drawings and paintings by Pre-Raphaelite artists.

Return to Henry Cole Wing and turn immediately up the Keramic Staircase, through the Silver Galleries to Room 68

Here **Alex Beleschenko** has created a delicate rythmic lattice of stars to commemorate the generosity of the donors Mr and Mrs A H Whitely. This complex and subtle work helps to provide a calm and pleasant atmosphere within the study area.

Go back downstairs and follow signs to the Main Gallery

Morris room

In 1865 **Henry Cole** invited the relatively unknown firm of **Morris Marshall Faulkner and Co** to decorate the Green Dining room, one of a series of refreshment rooms for the public. The stained glass was designed by **Edward Burne-**

Jones showing girls making garlands and playing musical instruments in a gentle Italianate context with background decorations on clear glass by William Morris.

Gamble room

Originally called the Centre Refreshment Room, its five large windows were decorated with a lively pattern of swags, ribbons, curlicues and inset heraldic emblems and scenes. These were fabricated by **Powells** between 1869 and 1871.

Poynter room

Here the decorations were designed by **Edward Poynter** and the stained glass made by **Crace and Sons**.

Continue to Northern Europe (28/29)

Several fine Renaissance windows can be  seen here including the series depicting the Royal House of Burgundy taken from the Chapel of the Holy Blood in Bruges. The portrait of Mary of Burgundy is particularly appealing. She is shown lifting her heavy damask dress to reveal the green silk beneath, while holding her pet dog in the crook of her elbow.

Continue on this level to Europe 1100 - 1450 (23/24)

The three figures from Winchester College Chapel are fine examples of the English work so much admired by Comper and his followers principally for the clarity of line painting and the use of white or clear glass.

Upstairs to find The National Art Library. Continue at this level past Lord Leighton's frescoes to the long gallery - room 111

This assorted collection of panels has been arranged by date and place. Treasures include a superb 'Triumph of Death' (1520) from the Church of St John in Rouen, and an exquisite fragment, a painted head of the 'Crowned Virgin' from East Anglia besides several

feathery medieval angels. The sloping
showcases allow people to examine paint,
stain and enamel technique in detail.
Look out for 'Labours of the Month' from
Cassiobury Park. Towards the end of the
Gallery the 'Tale of St George and the
Dragon' can be seen, a rare work in glass
by **Dante Gabriel Rossetti**.

How the good Knight St George of England slew the dragon and set the Princess free

Go straight ahead to room 112

Here the development of blown and kiln formed glass can be traced in several crowded showcases. There are some examples of interesting contemporary studio glass on display. The best thing here are the dramatic dangerous looking balustrades by **Danny Lane**.

Follow signs to view the **Dale Chihuly** *chandelier*

Go to rooms 116 and 117

These panels originally formed part of the decoration of several religious houses in Germany forcibly closed by Napoleon. They were brought to England and set into the Chapel of Ashridge Park. In 1928 they were given to the Museum. Look out for Tobias and Sarah lying in their four poster bed with their dog curled up at their feet.

Panels of stained glass can also be found in rooms 63 and 8

In the passage outside room 74 there is a roundel designed by **Roger Fry** at the **Omega Workshops** in 1914 and made by **Lowndes & Drury** for Lady Hamilton's house, 1 Hyde Park Gardens.

Return to the ground floor, to explore the fascinating Medieval Treasury Room, 43

Walk 6
Around Covent Garden

Start: Charing Cross
Finish: Holborn

A short walk which includes **Covent Garden Craft Market**. All the glass is twentieth century and almost all designed to improve a difficult building. **Brian Thomas** created additions to **St Paul's Church**, Covent Garden, **Brian Clarke** made new glass for the **Lavers and Barrauld Workshop**, while **Adelle Corrin** and **Kathy Shaw** transformed the stairwells at the **City Literary Institute**. The **Cochrane Gallery** above the **Cochrane Theatre** is now a well established exhibition space for contemporary architectural glass.

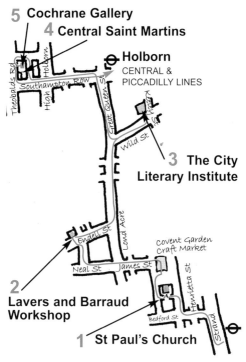

5 Cochrane Gallery

4 Central Saint Martins

Holborn
CENTRAL &
PICCADILLY LINES

Theobalds Rd
High Holborn
Southampton Row
Great Queen S
Kean St
Wild St

3 The City Literary Institute

Long Acre

Endall St

Covent Garden Craft Market

Neal St   James St

Henrietta St

2
Lavers and Barraud Workshop

Bedford St

Strand

1 St Paul's Church

Charing Cross
NORTHERN, BAKERLOO LINES
MAINLINE STATION

Walk 6

Around Covent Garden

1 **St Paul's Church**
Henrietta Street
Open Mon - Sat 10.00 - 4.00

2 **Lavers and Barraud Workshop**
Endell Street
Exterior view only

3 **The City Literary Institute**
Keeley Street
Mon - Fri Open 1.00 - 6.00
Ask at reception to view glass

Central Saint Martins College of Art & Design

Southampton Row
Exterior view on Fisher Street
from the Car Park
Tel (020) 7514 2000

Cochrane Gallery

Southampton Row
Open Mon - Fri 10.00 - 5.30
Sat - open during performances
Tel (020) 7242 7040

Refreshments

Covent Garden market area
Southampton Row and Theobalds Road
Cochrane Gallery Cafe

St Paul's Church

The windows made by **Brian Thomas**
between 1968-69 for the east end were
designed in conjunction with restoration
following war damage. Thomas was an
appropriate choice since his enthusiasm
for the Baroque period in art and his

practise as a mural painter fitted him well
for this task. Here he has created a pair
of elegant balanced windows using the
simplest means - clear glass, paint and
stain - to warm and lighten the interior.

2 **Lavers and Barraud Workshop**

Shorts Gardens

Neal St

Betterton St

Endell St

Long Acre

James St

King St   Covent Garden

Covent Garden Craft Market

Henrietta St

Bedford St

1 **St Paul's Church**

Strand

🚇 **Charing Cross**
NORTHERN, BAKERLOO LINES
MAIN LINE STATION

Lavers and Barraud Workshop

On Endell Street the exterior of the one time studio of the stained glass firm **Lavers and Baraud** has been preserved and the interior converted into offices. For the Boardroom, the brilliant young artist **Brian Clarke** was commissioned (with financial help from the Crafts Council) to create a contemporary window visible from outside as well as inside. Here he has

skilfully combined a very simple rhythmic pattern with dramatic flicks and interruptions, a counterpoint that he would examine further as his career progressed.

Commenting on his own work at this time he wrote 'I would make a grid of horizontal and vertical lines and break into the grid with a more fluid line, a more nervous line. And this of course, was something that I had already seen done in the work of Schreiter in Germany. Later it became apparent that here was a real area for exploration. It is this very interaction, this very electric dynamic opposition of forces that make life interesting, and certainly make art interesting'.

The City Literary Institute

The dull stairway inherited from the days when this building was a Primary School has been transformed by a series of glass windows created by **Adelle Corrin**. These  colourful abstract windows relate to the departments on each floor and were made between 1984 and 1990, as funds became available. They are just as effective at night when the entire sequence can be seen from outside the building.

In 1991 **Kathy Shaw** joined the teaching staff and made an additional window with input from students at the Institute for the Deaf.

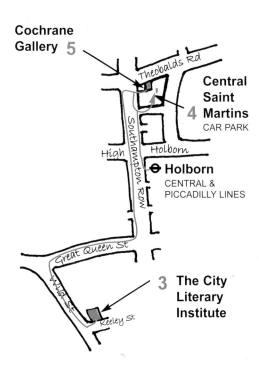

Cochrane Gallery 5

Theobalds Rd

Central Saint Martins 4
CAR PARK

High Holborn

⊖ **Holborn**
CENTRAL & PICCADILLY LINES

Southampton Row

Great Queen St

3 **The City Literary Institute**

Keeley St

Central Saint Martins College of Art & Design

While teaching at the nearby Central School of Art, **Tom Fairs** was commissioned to build an eye catching frieze in dalle de verre for the Foyer of the new **Polytechnic of Central London**, casting the blocks in the glass department opposite to be ready as the building went up.

He chose a dramatic colour scheme with a tough jazzy composition which was enormously effective as a marker for the Drake Street entrance. For the base he made a decorative low relief frieze which completes the exterior elevation.

Cochrane Gallery

Attached to the **Cochrane Theatre**, this Gallery has acquired a reputation as the place to see examples of new work in glass. Besides the work of students on the **Glass Courses** at **Central Saint Martins** and artists in the United Kingdom, shows have been brought to London from abroad, with substantial help from the London Arts Board. **Linda Lichtman** from the USA exhibited in 1997, **Tobias Kammerer** and **Helga Reay-Young** (pictured) both from Germany, in

1998-99. **Leifur Briedfjörd** from Iceland had a very successful show in 2000, and from Ireland, **Mary Mackey** in 2001.

Walk 7

Around Sloane Square & Bloomsbury

Start: Sloane Square
Continue: Goodge Street
Finish: Chancery Lane

This is an **Arts and Crafts** walk in two parts starting at **Holy Trinity, Sloane Street** to see the windows specially commissioned from **Edward Burne-Jones, Christopher Whall** and **William Blake Richmond.** A short underground journey to Goodge Street leads to the **University Church of Christ the King** to see **Lilian Pocock's** powerful figure windows. A fine late window by **Christopher Whall** can be seen in **Gray's Inn Chapel** and the walk ends with **Edward Nuttgens** masterpiece, the east window at St Etheldreda's Church, Ely Place.

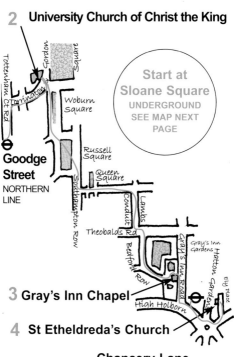

2 University Church of Christ the King

Tottenham Ct Rd

Gordon

Square

Torrington

Woburn Square

⊖ **Goodge Street**
NORTHERN LINE

Russell Square

Southampton Row

Queen Square

Start at
Sloane Square
UNDERGROUND
SEE MAP NEXT PAGE

Lambs

Conduit

Theobalds Rd

Bedford Row

Gray's Inn Road

Gray's Inn Gardens

Hatton Garden

Ely Place

3 Gray's Inn Chapel

High Holborn

4 St Etheldreda's Church

Chancery Lane
CENTRAL LINE

Walk 7

Around Sloane Square & Bloomsbury

1

Holy Trinity Church
Sloane Street
Open Mon - Fri 9.30 - 5.30
Sat - 10.00 - 5.00
Sun - services only

2

University Church of Christ the King
Gordon Square
Open Mon - Fri 10.00 - 4.00

3

Gray's Inn Chapel
Gray's Inn
Open Mon - Fri 10.00 - 6.00

4 St Etheldreda's Church
Ely Place
Open Daily 8.00 - 6.00

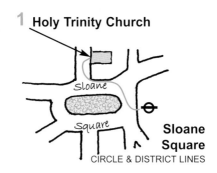

1 Holy Trinity Church

Sloane

Square

Sloane Square
CIRCLE & DISTRICT LINES

Refreshments

Off Sloane Square
between Russell Square and Queen Square
Lamb's Conduit Street and High Holborn

Holy Trinity

The church was designed by the architect
John Dando Sedding in 1888. Although
the style appears to be Gothic Revival,
Sedding transformed the interior of the
building by his enthusiasm for the decorative arts. He created opportunities for
sculpture, metalwork and stained glass
from artist members of the newly
formed Art Workers Guild of which he
was a founder member. His early death
prevented the completion of Holy Trinity
according to Arts and Crafts principles.

East window

Sedding planned both the east and west
windows with **Edward Burne-Jones** in
mind. However, only the east window
was completed. Burne Jones envisaged
this as 'filled with thousands of little
bright figures' within a background

designed by **William Morris**. The iconography of the window has been worked out with care. Within the traceries the 'Nativity' is at the head of the window surrounded by cherubs. Angels fill the lower traceries and the 'Acts of Mercy' fill the circle; deeds which have been interpreted as being performed by women. Above each set of four lancets which divide the great width of the window, there are three smaller scenes - the 'Crucifixion', the 'Fall' and the 'Annunciation'. Prophets, apostles and saints have been arranged in rows below, the uppermost being the 'Twelve Apostles' with Paul replacing Judas. In the second tier the patriarchs and prophets have been

7
walk

represented while the lower rows contain an assortment of saints several of which were specially designed for this window. All the figures are in silhouette upon a foliate background with a border of formalised sprigs around the edge.

For Burne Jones painting was his most important task. Stained glass designs were left for the evening. His wife Georgiana has given us some idea of his working methods in her book, 'Memorials' describing the 'large free drawings which came out upon the paper so quickly that it seemed as if they must have been already there and his hand only removing a veil.'

South side

The first window made by **Christopher Whall** was 'The Nativity' (1900). Here the originality and charm of his approach to stained glass can be appreciated. The interpretation of the subject - an outdoor scene with richly costumed participants -

still owes much to Burne-Jones. However, the thoughtful handling of the material, each piece of glass considered and worked upon by the artist designer gives a far more personal 'feel' to the window.

The second window, the 'Works of the Holy Spirit' (1906) shows Whall developing his own interpretation of christian iconography. Here the northern and southern churches have been suggested by the clothing of the onlookers who stand beside the Pentecost scene with its tongues of fire and rushing wind.

Particular attention in both windows has been paid to the border and background glass. Indeed the search for new effects was one of the distinguishing features of the Arts and Crafts movement in glass under Whall's direction.

Clerestory

These 'Angel' windows were added as funds became available. The last was completed in 1923. Whall had a colour code for the angelic hierarchy. The seraphim had red wings for love, the cherubim blue for wisdom whereas the purple winged angels linked love and wisdom. Here the figures float convincingly within the stone clerestory because Whall has most carefully judged the effect of colour and paint when seen from the distance below.

Whall's new approach to creating and making stained glass windows was consolidated in the running of his own studio where his assistants - many of them women- were treated as potential masters and encouraged in their own work. He was also involved in the setting up of classes in the newly established colleges of art and in this context wrote an influential

text book on the making of windows 'Stained Glass Work', a volume that remains unsurpassed.

North Side

These were designed by **William Blake Richmond** between 1905 and 1910. He was also a member of the Art

Workers Guild being Master in 1891. His grand, rather intense windows owe much to his work in mosaic for St Paul's Cathedral. They combine complex historical pictures in glass with superb and original decoration, strongly influenced by the man after whom he was named: William Blake. In these windows, which repay careful examination, Richmond avoids the obvious stories and presents unusual events in the lives of those he wishes to illustrate.

The central window shows scenes from

the boyhood of 'David, Samuel, Tobias and Daniel'. While those on either side depict male and female 'Virtues' accompanied by appropriate historical illustrations.

Richmond was a brilliant academic painter and Professor of Painting at the Royal Academy Schools. He also ful-filled important portrait commissions for Queen Victoria. For these windows he drew out full sized cartoons which were then taken to **Powells** for fabrica-tion. Despite this conventional approach, Richmond was enthusiastic about Arts and Crafts practise in glass observing that the division of labour was 'fatal to art' and that the designer should carry out his designs whenever it was pos-sible to do so.

From Sloane Square take the underground to Goodge Street. Cross Tottenham Court Road to Torrington Place. Keep straight ahead to reach Gordon Square. University Church is on the corner.

walk

University Church of Christ the King

(built as the Catholic Apostolic Church)

This church was built for members of the congregation of The Catholic Apostolic Church, a unique organisation founded in the 1830's with its own priestly hierarchy and orders of service. **Lilian Pocock** worshipped here and created several fine windows for the north side from 1930 onwards. She was trained both by Whall and by his brilliant pupil Karl Parsons who ran classes at the Central School of Art. She illustrated several books and this side of her artistic personality can be seen in these windows.

North side

The three windows on the north side have been set out in pairs. 'Moses and Aaron' 'David and Solomon', 'Elijah and John

the Baptist'. **Lilian Pocock** retained the same pictorial arrangement in each. Every window has a strong central figure with relevant scenes above and below and fascinating details within the border. She had evidently evolved her own method of painting on glass, working with different tools into unfired paint. This etched look gives her work its special depth and intensity. Her talent for illustration can

best be admired in the vivid and original way in which she interpreted well known Bible stories. Look for the Queen of Sheba in the 'King Solomon' window and the dramatic vignettes in the 'David' window.

In the Lady Chapel she made the 'Christ in Glory' with the four Evangelists at the east end. The other windows were added later to match her style by **Arthur Buss** of **Goddard and Gibbs**.

Cross to Woburn Square, then follow the map to the Inn's of Court gateway. Follow signs to Gray's Inn.

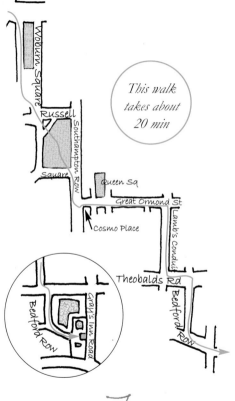

Woburn Square

This walk
takes about
20 min

Russell

Southampton Row

Square

Queen Sq

Great Ormond St

Cosmo Place

Lamb's Conduit

Theobalds Rd

Bedford Row

Bedford Row

Gray's Inn Road

7
Walk

Gray's Inn Chapel

Here **Christopher Whall** created a fine
and poignant memorial to the young men
of Gray's Inn who were killed in the First
World War. Whall chose as his subject a
trio of figures: 'St Louis', to represent
France, 'St George' for England, and the
warrior 'Archangel Michael'. All have
been shown in armour and given
emblems of identification - flag, shield,
sword and so on. Indeed Whall once

described the effort
it had taken him to
model a suit of
armour out of lay-
ers of paper in
order to improve
his ability to make
stained glass
armour convincing.
What distinguishes
these windows

from so many memorials made at the time is the absence of all sense of the heroic. Indeed, Whall has subtly underscored the terrible truth of the losses of that appalling war. These figures are children. Whall has given the sacred figures child shaped bodies and the painted heads of boys.

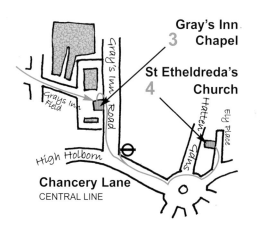

St Etheldreda's

In his youth Christopher Whall had been a lay
member of the Rosminian Order of Charity
based at St Etheldreda's and designed nave
windows for the church which were made for
him by WG Saunders in Endell Street. These
were destroyed during the Blitz. In the course
of the rebuilding programme, **Edward
Nuttgens** was asked to make a new east
window. He was 62 when he began and
took two years to complete the work.
Nuttgens had attended classes at the
Central School but learnt his craft mainly
through acting as assistant to Karl Parsons
at the Glasshouse in Fulham. He remained
true to the Arts and Crafts principles all his
life, doing all the work required in his own
studio at Piggots Hill in Buckinghamshire.

This rich and remarkable window shows
Nuttgens at his best. The strong simply
drawn figures owe much to the icono-
graphical manner of his friend Eric Gill

and provide the framework for wonderfully ebullient pattern making. His son, the stained glass artist, Joe Nuttgens, remembers the excitement his father felt in finding new colour combinations for the border and background.

The subject of this window includes

'Christ in Majesty', the 'Apostles', the 'Last Supper', 'St Etheldreda' herself and 'St Bridget'. Particularly successful are the robed angelic figures with their bright red halos and pale purple faces.

The artist, **Charles Blakeman** a friend of Nuttgens, made the more illustrative windows on the north and south side to match the colour and proportion of the east window. He also made the less successful west window and the glass in the crypt below.

Walk 8
Around the Inns of Court

Start: Embankment
Finish: Holborn

Timing is very important. A late start
will allow entry into the **Queen's Chapel**
where some fragments of Medieval glass
can be seen in detail. However, do not
loiter, as **Prince Henry's Room** and
Lincoln's Inn Chapel close at 2.00 and
2.30 respectively. **Sir John Soane's
Museum** contains the architect's collection of continental panels set into the
windows of his remarkable house.

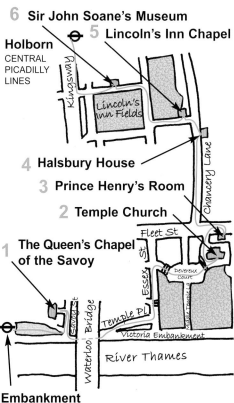

6 Sir John Soane's Museum

Holborn
CENTRAL
PICADILLY
LINES

5 Lincoln's Inn Chapel

Kingsway

Lincoln's
Inn Fields

Chancery Lane

4 Halsbury House

3 Prince Henry's Room

2 Temple Church

Fleet St

1 The Queen's Chapel
of the Savoy

Essex St

Devereux
Court

Savoy St

Waterloo Bridge

Temple Pl

Middle Temple Ln

Victoria Embankment

River Thames

Embankment
CIRCLE, DISTRICT, NORTHERN, BAKERLOO LINES

Walk 8

Around the Inns of Court

1

The Queen's Chapel of the Savoy
Savoy Hill
Open Tues - Fri 11.30 - 3.30
Sunday - service 11.00
Closed - Mon

2

Temple Church
Otpen Wed - Fri 11.00 - 4.00
Sat 11.00 - 2.30
Sun - Choral Mattins
Organ recital Wed 1.15 -1.45
Closed - Mon - Tues

3

Prince Henry's Room
Fleet Street
Open Mon - Sat 11.00 - 2.00

Halsbury House
35 Chancery Lane
Exterior view only

Lincoln's Inn Chapel
Lincoln's Inn
Open Mon - Fri 12.00 - 2.30
During Law Sittings

Sir John Soane's Museum
Lincoln's Inn
Open Tues -Sat 10.00 - 5.00
Free but donations welcome
Lecture Tour (£3.00) Sat 2.30
Closed - Mon

Refreshments

Fleet Street and Southampton Row

The Queen's Chapel of the Savoy

Medieval and **Tudor** glass, part of **Dr J F Gravling's** collection, was arranged sympathetically by **Joan Howson** during the

1950s in retained window openings which now form part of the choir vestry. It is possible with permission from the verger on duty to examine these wonderful examples of English glass in detail. Of particular interest are the donor figures of the knight and lady kneeling in readiness for the Last Judgement and the background of ornamental plant forms on clear glass admired for what came to be regarded as typically English qualities of lightness and simplicity.

Go Back down Savoy Street and left under Waterloo Bridge. Pass Somerset House, bear left on Temple Place then sharp left between bollards into Milford Lane and up steps into Essex Street. Turn right at the Edgar Wallace Pub into Devereux Court and through a gateway into New Court. Go down steps with the fountain on your right and pause to admire the heraldic windows in the Middle Temple Hall. Continue ahead under the arch into Elm Court then up steps into the square in front of Temple Church.

Temple Church

Following drastic wartime damage, six small panels are all that remain of **Thomas Willement's** revolutionary makeover of Temple Church between 1839-42. When completed, the Church was described as 'the most perfect metropolitan specimen of the eldentime'. These minute panels are worth examining in detail, however, since they reveal Gothic Revival sensibilities in glass in its very early stages.

Willement was an important influence in the early years of Queen Victoria's reign. He was a scholar, an antiquarian, a keen heraldic artist and friend of Charles Winston whose book 'Hints on Glass Painting' published in 1847 become the essential guide and handbook for all things Gothic in glass.

The Round

Later, and more flamboyant work, circa 1850, probably by **Henry Hughes** can be seen in the Round. Hughes had assisted Willement on windows for the Savoy Chapel. He later joined **Thomas Ward** to form the stained glass company **Ward and Hughes**

East end

In the mid 1950s the Worshipful Company of Glaziers sponsored a competition to design a new window for the east end to be judged by the Queen Mother. She chose **Carl Edwards'** design. The first windows were made with **Whitefriars**

Studio for whom Edwards was working as a designer . The others were completed in his own rented studio at the Apothecaries Hall in Blackfriars. The brilliant colour and mosaic-like feel to the window drew considerable praise from Sir Nicholas Pevsner. In London Vol 1 he described them as 'among the best post-war glass in London'.

Exit the Temple Church, turn right, then right again up narrow Inner Temple Lane.

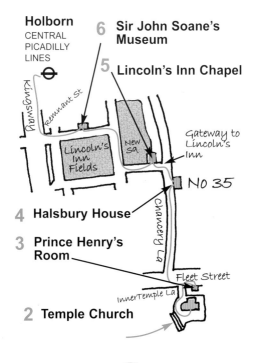

Holborn
CENTRAL
PICADILLY
LINES

6 **Sir John Soane's Museum**

5 **Lincoln's Inn Chapel**

Remnant St

Kingsway

Lincoln's Inn Fields

New Sq

Gateway to Lincoln's Inn

No 35

Chancery La

4 **Halsbury House**

3 **Prince Henry's Room**

Fleet Street

InnerTemple La

2 **Temple Church**

Prince Henry's Room

This is an upper room surviving from Tudor times bought for the nation by the **London County Council** in 1900. The heraldic stained glass was commissioned at this time from the firm **Burlison and**

Grylls. The LCC seal was designed by the remarkable artist **Walter Crane** an important figure in the Arts and Crafts movement. Largely self taught, his illustrations of fairy tales remain classics of their kind. He became principal of the Royal College of Art and wrote a number of textbooks: 'Line and Form', 'Ideals in Art'; which influenced the teaching of art and craft.

Halsbury House

The foyer window at 35 Chancery Lane, was designed by **Brian Clarke**. Here his ideas relating to formality and dynamism can be seen in the contrast between the grid and the amorphous shapes. This window was made at the **Derix Studios** at Taunusstein in Germany from a scale

design by Clarke. The glass itself is unusual in being coloured and yet semi-opaque, qualities that allow the composition to be seen and understood by artificial as well as natural light.

Lincoln's Inn Chapel

The east window has been entirely filled with coats of arms of the Treasurers of the Society from 1680 to the present day. The most recent have been made by **Caroline Benyon** daughter of Carl Edwards and herself a skilled glass worker.

For many years the Jacobean figure windows on the north and south side had been

assumed to be the work of **Bernard van Linge**. However, Michael Archer of the Victoria and Albert Museum recently discovered hidden monograms within the plinths of the windows depicting Saints Philip and Saint Bartholomew. He felt that these referred to

the English glass painter **Richard Butler.**
Archer further considers that Zacharias,
Ezekial and Jeremiah were made by
Bernard's brother **Abraham van Linge**. The
Dutch brothers came to England in 1621
and made stained glass windows for several
Oxford College chapels. Butler is known to
have worked for Robert Cecil, later Lord
Burghley, chief minister to Queen Elizabeth I.

Certainly there is evidence of considerable
variety of style. Butler's powerful apostles
seem to be bursting out of their window
space, Bernard Van Linge's saints move
tentatively across a watery landscape,
while Abraham's Patriarchs are costumed
in Jacobean dress.

This was an era of glass painting.
Coloured enamels as well as paints and
stain were used to get the effects
required. Particularly fascinating are the
ornate bases to these figure windows
filled with imaginative detail.

Sir John Soane's Museum

This Museum was once the home of the architect **Sir John Soane** (1753 - 1837). Here he lived and worked surrounded by his collection of sculpture, paintings and curiosities of all kinds. His stained glass panels were bought at auction and set into windows around the house. Their provenance remains uncertain but since most have a sacred subject it can be assumed that they were made for continental religious houses shut down by Napoleon.

Wandering round the house it can be seen that Soane used stained glass to accentuate the feeling of comfort in a room. He also used strips of reflecting mirror glass and lenses to light the dark places 'catching the lights and shades'. Soane often gilded his overhead skylights with yellow stain to bring a sense of sunshine into the space below.

An entirely different effect was aimed at in the basement crypt, the **Monk's Parlour** where 'Padre Giovanni' used to entertain his guests to tea. Here the red and blue bands of colour framing the painted glass pictures combine to enhance the sense of mystery within this slightly macabre place.

A few of the panels are worth examining in their own right. In the **Dining Room** there are two entertaining works

by an unknown Swiss artist made in 1600 in a lively naive style showing the 'Creation' and the 'Last Judgement' with the donor's family kneeling apprehensively on the ground.

walk 9

Around St Paul's

Start: Chancery Lane
Exit 3 Southside
Finish: St Paul's

This walk is devoted to the work of
Brian Thomas (1912-89), an accomplished artist whose painting and glass
so well suited the post-war reconstruction of **St Paul's Cathedral** and many
City Churches.

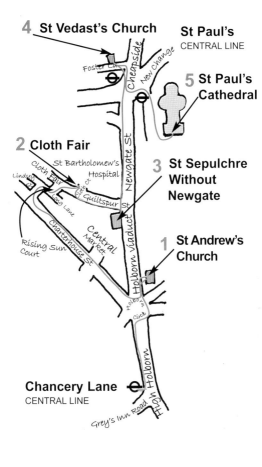

4 St Vedast's Church

St Paul's
CENTRAL LINE

Foster La.

Cheapside

New Change

5 St Paul's
Cathedral

2 Cloth Fair

St Bartholomew's
Hospital

Cloth Fair

Lindsey...

Newgate St

3 St Sepulchre
Without
Newgate

Giltspur St

Long Lane

Central Market

Charterhouse St

Rising Sun
Court

Holborn Viaduct

1 St Andrew's
Church

Holborn

Circus

Chancery Lane
CENTRAL LINE

High Holborn

Grey's Inn Road

Walk 9

Around St Paul's

1 **St Andrew's Church**
Holborn Viaduct
North entrance
Open Mon - Fri 10.00 - 5.00

2 **Cloth Fair**
Rising Sun Court
Exterior view only

3 **St Sepulchre Without Newgate**
Giltspur Street
Open Tues 12.00 - 2.30
Wed   11.00 - 3.00

4 St Vedast's Church
Foster Lane
Open Mon - Fri 8.00 - 6.00

5 St Paul's Cathedral
Open Mon - Sat 8.30 - 4.00
Admission charge
Sunday - services only

Refreshments

On High Holborn and Cheapside
St Paul's Cathedral (Crypt Refectory)

9 walk

St Andrew's Church Holborn

Brian Thomas designed two windows for this church, an east window and a small contemplative window for the separate lady chapel at the west end.

The window above the altar is profoundly theatrical. Here a curtain suspended from a crown has been looped back to reveal 'Christ's Last Supper' and 'Resurrection' in aerial perspective within gilded frames. These monochrome pictures have been flanked by outrageously enlarged heraldic cartouches. Thomas has used the time honoured method of setting out the design on a grid thus linking his composition with the clear glass windows on either side.

For the chapel, Thomas painted a dove - symbol of the Holy Spirit - flying out towards the viewer against a background of blazing light and parted cloud. An enigmatic note has been introduced by a

vase of wilting chrysanthemums and the
minute figure of a veiled woman who
indicates the turned pages of an enormous book for our attention.

*From Holborn Viaduct, cross to Charterhouse
Street. Walk past the Central (meat) Market.
Turn right on Lindsey Street, cross Long Lane
and go down narrow Rising Sun Court, which
leads to Cloth Fair. Look out for the blue plaque
to John Betjeman. The wall painting is nearby.*

Cloth Fair

Lord Mottistone and **Paul Paget** commissioned Thomas to paint this lighthearted picture on copper of a Victorian sailor boy returning to the bosom of his family to cover a window bricked up in the house opposite.

2 Cloth Fair

Go into West Smithfield, passing in front of St Bartholomew's Hospital. At the junction with Holborn Viaduct, cross Giltspur Street with care, then turn right to enter St Sepulchre by its second south door.

St Sepulchre Without Newgate

Thomas made two very fine windows for the **Musicians Chapel**. The 'Nellie Melba' window contains a large amount of information about the famous singer's life and career presented in an unusual and skilful way. Her portrait is rendered as if in

pastel and set in an oval frame surrounded by a wreath of nightingales. Peaches suggest the dessert (Pêche Melba) made in her honour by the chef Escoffier of the Ritz Hotel, London. Her operatic career has been commemorated in a series of small slate blue scenes. St Wilfred, patron of music, presides.

The window for 'John Ireland' has St John as patron saint looking for inspiration towards the vision of the Heavenly City. Ireland's own music has been set into the window as well as illustrations of his compositions which include 'Maidun, Satyricon, Songs of a Wayfarer, The Land of Lost Content and I had Six Cattle'. The border has been made out of small pieces of roughly textured glass which accentuate the delicacy of the vignettes.

Leaving St Sepulchre, turn left downhill on Newgate Street until you reach Foster Lane.

St Vedast

Thomas took the stories clustering around the 'Life of St Vedast', sorted out the scale of the principle figures (King Clovis and Queen Clotilde, St Remegius and St Aubert), added dramatic moments (Vedast healing a blind man and restoring the Roman Christian tombs) and filled the window with a rich background of flowers, fruit, sheaves of corn, birds and insects. Thomas' interest in symbols both old and new can be seen within these borders. Here there are references to incidents in Vedast's life, either his predilections (vine stems, glass and flask) or of his legend (occurrences concerning his shrine).

Around Clovis and Clotilde symbols of strength and submission have been placed opposite each other. The eagle and dove, the lamp of learning and the heart on fire, the lantern and the fountain, pelican and peacock, hart and dragon.

Thomas was a master of effect. His clever use of warm and cool glass enhanced with yellow and gold stain gives the east end of the church a shimmering presence.

From St Vedast cross Cheapside to enter St Paul's by the west end door.

walk

St Paul's Cathedral

East end

Brian Thomas was asked to create suitable glass to enhance a memorial to American servicemen who had died in the Second World War. From the west entrance the 'Crucifixion' can be seen while the predominant  colours echo those in W. B. Richmond's mosaic decorations.

The most important subject, 'Christ's Crucifixion', has been placed in the centre of the three commemorative windows. The treatment has been made deliberately emotional. Christ can be seen at the moment of death, his head drooped, his body slumped. Mary, the mother, has been literally pierced with her sorrow's sword. John, the friend, is distraught. Above this heartrending picture, the formal symbols used by Thomas to suggest Christian life: Pelican, Dove, Crown and Fountain have been placed one above the other, supported by putti, while below, the ark tosses on a stormy sea.

On either side the scenes build up to and away from the Crucifixion. On one side Christ washes his disciples feet and throws down the desecrators of the temple; in this context an analogy for the just use of force. On the other side Christ's Burial and Ascension have been shown. Each window has been given a border inset with American memorabilia and enhanced by flowers and fruit similar to those at St Vedast.

In the crypt and Order of the British Empire (OBE) Chapel

All the semi-basement windows contain glass by Thomas. The subject chosen was service: Christs command to his disciples to visit the sick, prisoners, take in strangers and feed the hungry. These were subjects that Thomas explored in greater depth for the north transept window in Westminster Abbey.

For the **OBE Chapel**, Thomas designed the metalwork and painted panels for the special enclosure. The royal portraits included those of **Queen Elizabeth II** and **Prince Philip** for which he was invited to Buckingham Palace for sittings. Getting lost one day, trying to find his way out, he told me he had spent an agreeable half hour 'in a room full of Rembrandts'.

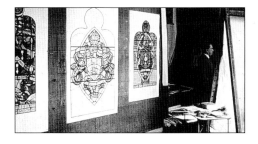

Walk 10

Around Cheapside

 Start: Cannon Street
Finish: St Paul's

A walk for those interested in post-war stained glass. **John Hayward**, **Lawrence Lee** and **Christopher Webb** all made fine windows for the restored City churches. An interesting example of **John Hutton's** engraved glass can be seen in the foyer of **Bucklersbury House** nearby.

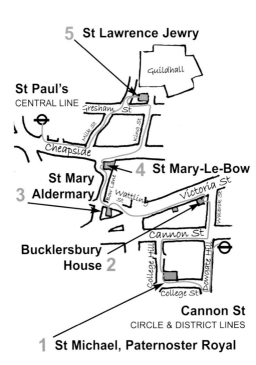

5 **St Lawrence Jewry**

Guildhall

St Paul's
CENTRAL LINE

Gresham St

Milk St

King St

Cheapside

St Mary-Le-Bow **4**

St Mary
Aldermary
3

Bow Lane

Wattling St

Victoria St

Walbrook

Cannon St

Bucklersbury
House **2**

College Hill

Dowgate Hill

College St

Cannon St
CIRCLE & DISTRICT LINES

1 **St Michael, Paternoster Royal**

Walk 10

Around Cheapside

1

St Michael, Paternoster Royal
(Missions to Seafarers)
College Hill
Open Mon - Fri 8.00 - 5.30

2

Bucklersbury House
Queen Victoria Street
Exterior view and reception

3

St Mary Aldermary
Watling Street
Open Mon - Fri 11.00 - 3.00
Mon, Thur 1.00 Service

4   **St Mary-Le-Bow**
Bow Lane
Open Mon - Fri 8.00 - 5.00

5   **St Lawrence Jewry**
Gresham Street
Open Mon, - Fri 7.00 -12.00
Wed 8.30 Service

Refreshments

Cannon Street, Cheapside, Bow Lane and
St Mary-le-Bow (The Place Below)

St Michael Paternoster Royal

This was one of the last churches to be rebuilt after the war. The architect was **Elidir Davis** and all the stained glass (1968-9) by **John Hayward**. The trio of windows at the east end has the entirely appropriate post-war subject of the 'Triumph of Good over Evil'. The central window shows the archangel Michael chaining Satan, the defeated rebel angel. On one side, a many headed red dragon attacks a mother and child, but the child

(filled with mystical power) rams a spear down the dragon's throat. On the other side Adam and Eve sitting under the apple tree are tempted by the serpent and rescued by the angel of the Annunciation. Hayward's stylised elongated figures show links with contemporary painting and sculpture, especially Henry Moore, John Hutton and Graham Sutherland.

The window near the door is a memorial to the one time benefactor of this church Dick Whittington - three times Lord Mayor of London - and his cat.

Bucklersbury House

The discovery of a Roman Temple to
Mithras beneath the rubble of Victoria
Street was the inspiration for the engraved

glass panels by the New Zealand-born artist
John Hutton. He had already worked out
the techniques that brought him fame - the
free cutting and engraving of the tough but
delicate surface of sheet glass. Here
Hutton has combined his enjoyment of
working with the human figure with interest in the Roman past. The central
Mithraic Sacrifice has been taken directly
from a stele now on show in the Museum

of London. The attendant figures include the Mithraic celebrants and personifications associated with the classical world - the 'Fates and Gods'. The most delightful of these are the reclining female figures of 'Air and Earth'.

Hutton's tenacity and daring lifted the art of engraving from a studio craft to an art suitable for innovative architectural enhancement.

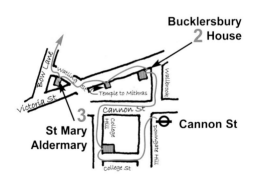

St Mary Aldermary

Insufficient money was allowed by the War Damages Commission to replace all the stained glass in St Mary, so the east, west and side chapel windows were ordered and the rest plain-glazed with heraldic additions. **Lawrence Lee** took over as artist in charge following the death of his colleague **Martin Travers**. Travers' influence is apparent in the first two windows. The simplified figures in strong outline within a clear glass background all recall his uncompromising approach. At the same time Lee took over the running of the glass department at the Royal College of Art where, over the years, so many artists were inspired to work in glass and where the great windows for Coventry Cathedral were made during the late 1950s.

East window

The two main scenes show the 'Annunciation' and 'Crucifixion', the beginning and end of Mary's role as Christ's Mother. The saints in attendance, St Nicholas and St Anthony represent the other parishes amalgamated with this church. Mary's mystical attributes with latin inscriptions form a band on either side. However, the row of scenes at the base illustrating different moments in Mary's life with Christ are particularly interesting, revealing Lee's growing interest in the interaction between the sacred and the ordinary in his art.

West window

This was made in 1950 with **John Crawford** as technical assistant. It has a simple post-war theme. The figures represent splendour and triumph while the buildings destroyed in the Blitz have been commemorated in a tapestry of towers along with the badges of the defending organisations.

Chapel window

Here Lee worked to his own design, mixing the sensitive representation of sacred individuals - 'Mother and Child', 'St Thomas' and 'St John the Baptist'- with an original approach to the essentials of a commemorative architectural work. The brief for this window required the inclusion of a reference to the rebuilder of the original church - Sir Christopher Wren. Here the relationship between the sacred figures has a certain diffident charm while the integration of Wren and his history into the composition has been accomplished with considerable wit.

Lee certainly considered himself an upholder of the Arts and Crafts tradition.

He designed, cut and painted his windows with assistance from his students whom he trained and often found work for. Alan Younger, Jane Gray, Tim Lewis, Ray Bradley, Geoffrey Clarke and Keith New among many others benefited from his support.

Exit the church, cross Watling Street, go up Bow Lane to Bow churchyard.

St Mary-Le-Bow

Postwar reconstruction was carried out by the architect **Lawrence King** who involved **John Hayward** in plans for the redecoration of the interior. Hayward designed the organ case, altar, pulpit and reredos and filled the windows with a

powerful and judgmental version of 'Christ in Majesty' based on the Book of Revelations. Flanking windows contain the austere and melancholy figures of 'St

Paul' and 'St Mary'. The background has been filled with references to the bombed churches of the City each with its patron saint. The forcefulness of these windows acts as a fierce counter-point to the gilded furnishings below.

The windows at the west end are entirely different in spirit. Rich in colour and full of information, they have been carefully arranged to create a satisfactory pattern of colour while retaining all the information required to represent what Hayward called the 'government of the City'

Chapel

An outside stairway leads down to a tiny secluded chapel. The angels engraved on the doors and the painted altar piece were both the work of Hayward, completed during his period of employment with the firm **Faithcraft**.

Walk

St Lawrence Jewry

With the exception of a roundel by **Lawrence Lee**, all the stained glass in this church is by **Christopher Webb** whose style entirely suits the elegant interior of this church rebuilt by the architect **Cecil Brown** after gutting by fire in the Blitz of 1940. Webb was trained first as an artist at the Slade then became articled to the architect Sir Ninian Comper. He developed Comper's style to suit his own more illustrative turn of mind. Webb's art, like Comper's, is essentially the art of drawing. Both made clear detailed scale designs backed up by careful research. A simple range of colour was adhered to - red, blue, light purple and green. Paint was applied in outline with minimal shading and the entire fabrication process carried out by competent craftsmen.

These were essentially decorative windows and entirely different from those that grew within the Arts and Crafts movement.

Entrance

This is a wonderful example of Webb's illustrational skills. His sympathetic commemoration of the builders and rebuilders of the church has been enhanced by the incidental scenes showing men engaged in all kinds of work including the fabrication of his own windows.

Walk

Webb took his cue for colour and decoration from the interior furnishings of the original building, in particular the twisting foliate metalwork of the Mayor's sword rest and the chandeliers. These elegant shapes provided the basis for the ornamental framework which he  used to surround each of his figures.

Indeed there is a suggestion of jewellery about these settings, with the figure as precious stone. Webb has placed each figure subject in a clearly defined central area, allowing plenty of clear glass all around so that the interior could be as light as possible.

The two windows on either side of the altar are the most elaborate in the church. Here 'St Paul' and 'St Catherine' stand with their emblems of martyrdom within a deep foliate border studded with heraldic shields. At the base of both

windows angels hold an image of the church. A sad angel grasps the burning building complete with searchlights and bombers. A happy angel presents the completed and restored church.

Here a light effect has been achieved with the masterly ordering of the heraldic emblems of the Sovereign Independent States which comprised the Commonwealth in 1957 (the year that the church was restored). The Crucifixion scene at the east end is a typical example of Webb's calm and clear approach to drama. Even the instruments of torture have been denied their unpleasant associations being arranged as a decorative border.

South side

The five windows along the wall each contain a single figure representing some aspect of the church's history. 'St Mary Magdalene', for example, commemorates the church in Milk Street united with St Lawrence in 1892.

Walk 11
Around the City

 Start: Monument
Finish: Liverpool Street

The **Victorians** renovated the City
churches with strenuous enthusiasm.
They used stained glass to give a romantic 'dim religious light' to the newly
enriched, interiors. Although emulation
of medieval piety led to the creation of
stained glass windows based on gothic
sources, other stylistic references were
apparently acceptable. Seeing one
scheme after another on this walk it is
possible to gain some insight into the
Victorian approach.

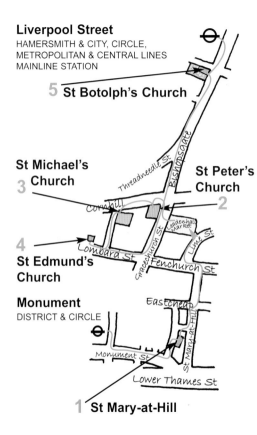

Liverpool Street
HAMERSMITH & CITY, CIRCLE,
METROPOLITAN & CENTRAL LINES
MAINLINE STATION

5 St Botolph's Church

St Michael's
3 Church

St Peter's
2 Church

4

St Edmund's
Church

Monument
DISTRICT & CIRCLE

1 St Mary-at-Hill

Threadneedle St
Bishopsgate
Cornhill
Leadenhall Market
Lime St
Lombard St
Gracechurch St
Fenchurch St
Eastcheap
Monument St
St Mary-at-Hill
Lower Thames St

Walk 11

Around the City

1 **St Mary-at-Hill**
Lovat Lane
Open Mon - Fri 11.00 - 4.00

2 **St Peter's Church**
Cornhill - Attached to Great
St Helen's
Call to check opening
(020) 7283 2231

3 **St Michael's Church**
Cornhill
Open Mon - Fri 9.30 - 2.00

4

St Edmund's Church
Lombard Street
Open Mon - Fri 10.00 - 4.00

5

St Botolph's Church
Bishopsgate
Open Mon - Fri 8.00 - 5.45
Wed, Fri 1.00 Service

From Monument Underground go down Fish Street Hill. Go left on Monument Street and turn left up Lovat Lane. St Mary-at-Hill will be on your right.

Refreshments

Leadenhall Market, Bishopsgate
Liverpool Street Station

Walk 11

St Mary-at-Hill

All that remains of the stained glass from the nineteenth century renovation (1848-49) are the borders in the windows on

the north side. These are of considerable interest since they reveal the extent to which medieval glass was copied during the early years of the Gothic Revival usually through the medium of Charles Winston's book 'Hints on Glass Painting'. Here we can see the 'scrolls of foliage which are not formed out of one continuous tendril, but of a series of short stalks or leaves'; described in this book in the chapter on Early English Glass. Coloured and diapered background also conform to Winston's description.

Leave St Mary-at-Hill by the north door and go through the alley to turn left into St Mary at Hill. Cross Eastcheap and go along Rood Lane. Cross Fenchurch Street and continue up Lime Street to Leadenhall Market. Go through the market to Gracechurch Street and turn down Cornhill. St Peter's Church is on the corner.

Walk

St Peter's Church

The complete scheme for the east end
was made in 1872 by **Charles Alexander
Gibbs** brother of Alexander Gibbs who
made the windows for All Saints,
Margaret Street.

Scenes which showed the 'Divinity of
Christ' were popular in post Darwinian
ecclesiastical circles. Here the 'Epiphany',
'Baptism', 'Crucifixion', 'Resurrection'
and 'Foundation of the Church on

Earth' have been supported by upper scenes featuring the 'Ascension' and 'Two Miracles'.

It is interesting to note that one of these, the 'Miraculous Draught of Fishes' has been copied carefully from the cartoon of the same subject by Raphael intended for the Sistine Chapel. This drawing would at that time have been known from engravings. However, the original was in the possession of Queen Victoria who gave the cartoon to the South Kensington Museum (now the V&A) where it would have been available, and still is on display for study.

From St Peter's, turn left on Cornhill. St Michael's Church is nearby.

St Michael Cornhill

The architect **George Gilbert Scott** reconstructed this church in the Italian Gothic style in the 1850s. He changed the window openings, decorated the plain walls and ordered stained glass from his two young assistants **John Clayton** and **Alfred Bell**. Bell, the younger of the two, was the gifted son of a Devon farm labourer who began working for Scott at the age of 14. Clayton's background was more conventional. He trained in sculpture at the Royal Academy schools, and worked for a couple of architects before joining Scott. Scott encouraged the two young men to set up their own business promising them plenty of work. Indeed almost all the buildings by or renovated by Scott have glass and furnishings by Clayton and Bell.

West window

This tall narrow window was designed by **Alfred Bell** when he was still in his twenties. It is a 'Crucifixion' scene in the Medieval manner. The figures have been elongated and formalised, their clothes and faces painted in the simple linear way recommended  by Charles Winston. This sombre but splendid window has been enriched by typical Clayton and Bell beds of flowers and a border in an intricate knot pattern.

East window

In marked contrast to the west window, this is a triumphant, almost a happy

window. Christ floats towards the congregation through a rainbow of minute
cherubs surrounded by angels playing
antique stringed instruments. The deep
border is quite oriental in its mix of foliate and geometric forms. Here the

source of imagery seems rather more Renaissance than Gothic. 'Christ Risen in Majesty' remained a potent subject for east windows throughout the Victorian period.

South side

These four windows were designed to be seen in chronological order starting at the west end. 'Epiphany' then 'Baptism'' 'Ministry' then 'Betrayal'. Of these, the 'Epiphany' is the most satisfactory. At the base there are two scenes: the 'Annunciation' and the 'Kings with Herod' which summarise the competent use of the updated Gothic formula. Unfortunately the background patterning to these windows was removed when the windows were reglazed and 'improved' to let light in during the 1930s so it is impossible to appreciate the total effect of the stained glass.

However, when the church was finished, the *Illustrated London News* published an engraving of the interior with an enthusiastic article in which the windows were described as: 'well drawn' and 'with a great display of brilliant colours.....exceedingly pure and in parts almost gemlike'.

Turn left down an alley beside the church to emerge on Lombard Street. St Edmund's Church is on the right.

St Edmund's Church

A rare surviving window by **James Powell and Sons**. This strange dark monumental work combines the 'Judging of the Twelve Tribes' with two subsidiary scenes, the 'Legends of St Nicholas and St Edmund'. Chapter 4 of the Book of Revelations was the source for the main subject which has been illustrated in all its complexity. The 'Legends' are in an entirely different visual language. St Nicholas has been shown giving golden balls to dowerless girls while St Edmund undergoes a macabre martyrdom.

Powell's were an important firm in the Victorian era. The founders **James** and **Harry Powell** were enthusiastic innovators. They made both flat and ornamental glass for William Morris and created mosaic pieces including those for

WB Richmond's designs in St Paul's Cathedral. The firm made their own stained glass windows. Burne-Jones and Henry Holiday both designed for them. The firm survived as **Whitefriars** until the 1970s.

Turn left on Lombard Street and left again on Gracechurch Street. Keep straight ahead along Bishopsgate to reach St Botolph's.

St Botolph Bishopsgate

In 1869 two windows were added
designed by **Frank Moody** and made by
Powells. Moody was a remarkable man.
He assisted Godfrey Sykes on the architectural decoration of what was then the
South Kensington Museum, designing
and making the Keramic staircase with
his students. He wrote an enormously
influential book on teaching, 'Lectures
and Lessons in Art' which was first published in 1880, going into five editions.
He also revived the ancient art of plaster
sgraffito which he used to decorate the
outside of the Royal College of Organists
and the exterior of the Science School.

East window

This 'Crucifixion' window, the only work
in glass to have survived by Moody

Walk 1

remains mysterious. Christ on the cross, flanked by John and Mary has been placed within an ornamental stage set with twisted pillars. Mary Magdalene can be seen distraught with her arms out-stretched. However, the Soldier Knight, the Martial Saint leaning on a wheel, the Apostle engrossed in his book and the girl who looks towards the congregation resist certain identity. In the brilliant blue sky, Moody has placed several grieving angels and the sun and moon.

The entire picture has been framed by an arch drawn in wonderfully convincing perspective, which acts as a device to link the scene to the wall of the chancel. Upon this stained glass architectural shape there are rosettes, swags, flowers and grotesques all of which help to give the composition its theatrical air.

Moody was drawn towards classical art. He also admired the work of William Blake and the perfectionist designer of Wedgwood's ceramics, John Flaxman.

Walk1

Walk 12
Around Fenchurch Street

Start: Aldgate
Then: Tower Hill
Finish: Whitechapel

This weekday walk includes glass spanning three centuries. There is a rare C17 rose window in **St Katherine Cree**. **St Botolph's** has an early Victorian window and modern additions by **Sally Scott** and **David Peace**. **St Olave's** has postwar glass by **Arthur Buss** and **John Hayward**. **All Hallows** has Baptistry glass by **Keith New**. Nearby there are two modern glass installations in office buildings by **Brian Clarke** and **Graham Jones**. Go two stops by underground to view windows on medical and scientific themes by **Johannes Schreiter** at the **Library of Barts & the London School of Medicine,** Whitechapel.

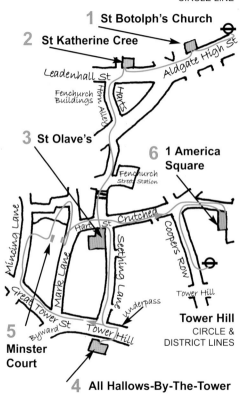

Aldgate
CIRCLE LINE

1 St Botolph's Church

2 St Katherine Cree

Aldgate High St

Leadenhall St

Fenchurch Buildings

Horn Alley

Harts

3 St Olave's

6 1 America Square

Fenchurch Street Station

Crutched

Mincing Lane

Hart St

Cooper's Row

Seething Lane

Mark Lane

Great Tower St

Byward

Tower Hill

Underpass

Tower Hill

Tower Hill
CIRCLE &
DISTRICT LINES

5
Minster
Court

4 All Hallows-By-The-Tower

Walk 12

Around Fenchurch Street

1 **St Botolph's Church**
Aldgate
Mon - Fri 10.00 - 4.30

2 **St Katherine Cree**
Leadenhall Street
Mon - Fri 10.30 - 4.30

3 **St Olave's Church**
Hart Street
Mon - Fri 10.00 - 5.00
(020) 7488 4318

4 **All Hallows-by-the-Tower**
Byward Street
Mon - Sat 10.00 - 4.00

Minster Court
Mincing Lane
Reception area only

 1 America Square
Reception area only

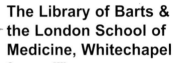 **The Library of Barts &
the London School of
Medicine, Whitechapel**
Stepney Way
Mon - Fri 9.00 - 6.00
Sat 9.00 - 12.00
Call to check
(020) 7882 7110

Refreshments
Fenchurch Street Station area
and within Minster Court

 Walk 12

St Botolph's Church

This church has found a worthy if difficult role where East End and City meet. Inside all is polished and warm; downstairs a meal is provided for 300 homeless people every evening.

East end

An important window by **Charles Clutterbuck** can be seen above the altar which marks the transition between the eighteenth century method of using paintings as a source for stained glass and the Victorian enthusiasm for new glass based on a creative version of the old. Here the painting by Rubens of 'Christ's Deposition' has been copied as carefully as possible. However, the flanking windows reveal an entirely different approach. These are complex mosaic windows in the new style. Clutterbuck was a friend of Charles Winston and it is tempting to speculate that in these we see the early beginnings of the influence of his interest in the Medieval past.

Chapel

The glass enclosing this small chapel has been decorated by two distinguished engravers. **David Peace** designed the inscriptions for the doors and **Sally Scott** made the evocative scenes which include the 'Ark, Phoenix and Dove'. The glass has been sandblasted, etched and engraved in a way that gives privacy yet keeps a sense of light within the interior.

St Katherine Cree

The church was rebuilt between 1628-31, unscathed by either the Fire or the Blitz. The stained glass in the rose or Catherine Wheel window at the east end was installed as part of this building.

East window

The surprising thing about this early seventeenth century glass is its freshness. The clear colours and abstract pattern are qualities that tend to be associated with our own time.

Originally the glass in the openings below would have contained the Royal (and loyal) coat of arms. However in 1876 the present splendid ornamental window was installed to commemorate the tradition of an annual Flower Sermon.

North and south side

Other additions to the church are mixed. There are fragments of heraldic cartouches, a pleasant St Cecilia window (1866), and a memorial window by **Michael Farrer Bell** (1963).

St Olave's Church

The church was badly damaged during the Blitz and restored with Norwegian associations in mind. The patron Saint Olave or Olaf had converted Norway to Christianity when he became King in 1015.

East end

Arthur Buss, chief designer at the London firm **Goddard and Gibbs** was given the task of replacing an earlier window above the altar by Francis Spear which was destroyed in the war. Buss took elements of the original subjects

(Resurrection and Ascension) in his depiction of 'Christus Salvator' and 'Christus Victor'. The Norwegian links were suggested by the inclusion of Saint Olaf as well as St George with the north sea flowing between them. The man-headed dragon refers to Olaf's difficulties with the conquest of 'the evil within himself'.

The window nearby, dedicated to 'Holy Women' is typical of so many produced during the immediate postwar period. Set within light glass, the figures have been shown as representatives of English virtues triumphant at this time. Here Mary in her role as 'Queen of Heaven' has been flanked by St Catherine and Queen Elizabeth I. Buss has placed historically important women above; Elizabeth Fry, Florence Nightingale, Josephine Butler and Edith Cavell. Arthur Buss worked as chief designer for Goddard and Gibbs until the 1960s. His output during the postwar period was prodigious. Between 1949-61 he designed windows for 156 churches as far afield as Africa, New Zealand and Ceylon. His designs would be worked out to  scale in watercolour and then drawn out full size in pencil and charcoal on cartoon paper. The glass would be cut for him using the design as guide and then completed from the cartoon.

North and South windows

The tinted glass for these windows has been chosen with unusual sensitivity and ornamented with heraldic shields. **John Hayward** added a window over the door in 1964 in which his lively interpretation of heraldry can be appreciated.

All Hallows-by-the-Tower

The architects **Lord Mottistone** and **Paul Paget** rebuilt the church after the Second World War, keeping the interior light. A fine painted reredos was commisioned from Brian Thomas. Some of the stained glass was rescued from the church and set for the sake of colour and historical association into the clear glazed windows. More heraldic glass was added over the years to commemorate local events, the most recent being on the south side.

Baptistery

The windows here were made by **Keith New** in 1964. They represent the lovely flowering of expression that occurred in stained glass after the completion of Coventry Cathedral. Mrs de Selincourt had seen New's windows there and gave him a free hand for these memorials to her husband Martin.

New has linked the principal subjects of 'Mother and Child' and 'St Martin' with appropriate supportive symbols - fish, boat, book and stringed instruments. His sense of colour remains one of his great contributions to the craft. Here

there is a lively play between the different greens he chose for one window and the golds and reds of the other. New applied paint in an updated version of Arts and Crafts methods, rubbing and scratching the pigment to emphasize form and create texture and using the brush to thicken leads, turning them

into boldly drawn lines. His background in graphics and his experience of working on the Coventry windows at the Royal College gave him the confidence to cut through traditional ways of thinking and so to use glass, paint and lead in a truly innovative way.

Return to Great Tower Street, turn left then right on Mincing Lane. Go up steps into the glass roofed complex of Minster Court.

Minster Court

This 1980s office development occupies a
substantial corner site off Mincing Lane.
After the building had been finished,
Graham Jones was asked to create a focal
point for the entrance to **2 Minster Court.**
Having considered the idea of sculpture,
ones settled on the concept of the circle to
hold the attention of people passing
through the portal. He chose rich translucent colours; dark ultramarine and pale

cobalt blue with notes of orange and scarlet. He decorated the glass with a mix of screen printed images and spatterings of paint.

The time scale for this window was just ten weeks. It was fabricated in Germany at **Derix Studios** in Taunusstein where Jones stayed, supervising the work and painting the glass himself.

After seeing the roundel, turn right and look for the down escalator to Dunster Court. Turn right on Mark Lane. The rear entrance of **2 Minster Court** *is on Mark Lane. Here there is another window by* **Graham Jones.**

Go back up Mark Lane. Turn right on Hart Street and continue straight along Crutched Friars. At the junction with Crosswall Street turn right. **1 America Square** *is on the right.*

1 America Square

This building, designed by architects **Renton, Howard, Wood & Levine** for the Nomura Bank, is one of the most spectacular put up during the Thatcher years. **Brian Clarke** was called in near completion to design glass for the centre of the foyer. Clarke has contrasted the blacks and greys of the marble clad interior with a sophisticated back lit panel. A grid of sliced onyx, cut to expose the beauty of the natural patterning of the stone has been set above another grid of gold and silver squares; a reference to the money market housed at that time within the building. Here ribbons of colour seem to spring across the formal ground. Clarke has nicked the edges with tiny buds to fix them to the frame. His colours relate to contemporary fashion and design in a way that gives this discreet yet opulent space exactly the focus that it needs.

Walk back down Crosswall Street, turn left on Coopers Row to reach Tower Hill Underground. Take the District Line east to Whitechapel.

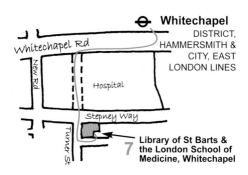

The Library of St Barts and the London School of Medicine, Whitechapel

The library is used by medical students and staff. Visitors are permitted to view the interior of the building but should respect the context. Opening times can vary according to the academic year.

Originally the church of St Augustine with St Philip, the building became redundant in 1979 and was later converted for use as a Library for the combined Medical Schools of the Royal London and St Bartholomew's Hospitals. Inspired by **Johannes Schreiter's** designs for the Heiliggeist Church in Heidelberg which included imagery derived from scientific sources, eight stained glass windows were commissioned over a ten year period on subjects

connected with contemporary medical
research and the history of the Royal
London Hospital.

Within the Library, the subjects for
the windows on the north side are 'The
London Hospital', 'AIDS',
'Gastroenterology' and 'Ethics'. Those
on the south side are 'Medical Diagnosis',
'Virology', 'Molecular Biology' and a

memorial to 'The Elephant Man':
Joseph Merrick.

Schreiter's superb understanding of
the medium has enabled him to create a
unified ensemble to enhance this difficult
building, coordinating a number of dis-
parate but immensely important
themes within the overall plan. These
windows are particularly important in
view of Schreiter's influence on the
development of glass in Britain. Here
the linear quality of the lead line can
be observed, as well as the absence of

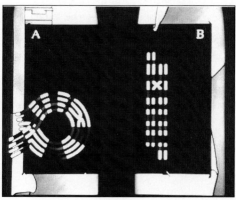

any supporting or enclosing features and the extraordinary control of colour.

Schreiter's contribution, however, has been less about technical innovation than intellectual appraisal. His clear minded assessment of all the elements of which this medium is made has given students of his work considerable insight into their own art. This analytical approach has undoubtedly enabled many young artists to understand the limitations of inherited solutions while suggesting ways for them to create new works of their own.

The windows were fabricated at **Derix Studios** at Taunusstein in Germany.

Walk 13
Southwark & Blackfriars

Start: Monument
Finish: Blackfriars

A wonderful walk for a fine day with views of London across the Thames and the chance to stop and see the Globe Theatre or the new Tate Modern on the way. Southwark Cathedral, one of the loveliest ecclesiastical interiors in London, has remarkable glass by **Henry Holiday, John La Farge, Ninian Comper, Christopher Webb, Lawrence Lee, Alan Younger** and **Benjamin Finn**. Lee's work can also be seen at St Magnus Martyr. At the end of the river walk, **John Lawson's** panels for the Daily Express at Ludgate House are visible. While on the far side of Blackfriars Bridge there's **Amber Hiscott's** glass for Unilever and two fascinating projects by **Brian Clarke**.

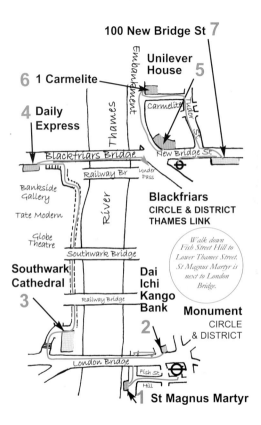

100 New Bridge St **7**

Unilever House **5**

Embankment

6 **1 Carmelite**

Thames

Carmelite

Tudor St

4 Daily Express

New Bridge St

Blackfriars Bridge

Railway Br

Under Pass

Blackfriars
CIRCLE & DISTRICT
THAMES LINK

Bankside Gallery

River

Tate Modern

Globe Theatre

*Walk down
Fish Street Hill to
Lower Thames Street.
St Magnus Martyr is
next to London
Bridge.*

Southwark Bridge

Southwark Cathedral

Dai Ichi Kango Bank

3

Railway Bridge

2

Monument
CIRCLE & DISTRICT

London Bridge

Fish St Hill

1 **St Magnus Martyr**

Walk 13

Southwark & Blackfriars

1

St Magnus Martyr
Lower Thames St
Mon - Fri 10.00 - 4.00

2

Dai Ichi Kango Bank
King William St
Exterior view only

3

Southwark Cathedral
Cathedral St
Mon - Sat 10.00 - 4.30
Sunday - services only

4 **Daily Express**
Ludgate House
Reception area only

5 **Unilever House**
Foyer view only

6 **1 Carmelite**
Carmelite St
Exterior and foyer view only

7 **100 New Bridge Street**
Exterior and foyer view only

Refreshments

Southwark Cathedral, on Bankside,
at Tate Modern, on New Bridge Street

1walk

St Magnus Martyr

North side

Some fragments of **C17** glass can be seen
made up into a panel. The colourful
heraldic windows, arms of various City
Livery Companies, were added during the
1950s by **Alfred L Wilkinson**.

South side

Lawrence Lee
made these win-
dows between 1950
- 52 using the tradi-
tional arrangement
of a single standing

figure within an architectural frame
against a clear glass background. Saints
'Magnus, Margaret, Thomas' and the
'Archangel Michael', are all dressed in
costumes that link them to the period in

which they lived. Lee has presented them as formidable human beings rather than sanctified types. Each plinth has been decorated with scenes from their life or the history of the church and parish.

Particularly endearing is St Magnus' church in Orkney with its ruined tower and flower studded grassy bank. Apart from his students' assistance, Lee made these windows himself which accounts for the charm of the painted figures.

For Lee, glass painting remained a matter of fundamental importance. In his seminal book 'The Appreciation of Stained Glass' he wrote 'After 30 years of struggle I still find myself baffled by the intricacies of this skill.'

Turn left, go up the steps and cross to the far side of London Bridge through the pedestrian underpass. Look up to see the office staircase windows.

Dai Ichi Kango Bank

John Lawson of **Goddard and Gibbs** designed the **staircase windows** in a bold abstract pattern using glass which would conceal the view of the interior during the day and yet give a cheerful message at night. Lawson used opaque glass for the largest shapes and a range of subtle translucent greens and golds to colour the

light shining into the stairwell. The basis of the design was a grid taken from the building itself interrupted by more dynamic motifs in order to create an upward spiralling movement within the window space. This project won the Art and Work Award for 1990.

Walk over London Bridge. On the far side turn right to Southwark Cathedral.

Southwark Cathedral

Originally part of a monastic foundation
the building became a Cathedral of the
Church of England in 1905.

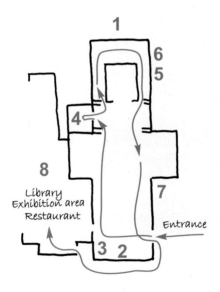

1

6
5

4

8

Library
Exhibition area
Restaurant

7

Entrance

3 2

1 The architect **Ninian Comper** had already restored the stone screen and added an altar to the east end when, at the age of 83, he designed the 'Christ in Glory' in the three windows above to replace a Crucifixion blown out in the Blitz.

Comper shows Christ eternally young with John the Baptist and Mary on either side. Large doves play around His outstretched hands. The colour of this window is outrageously strong. There are deep red, gold, green and violet shades of glass against an improbable prussian blue sky. But in Comper's hands these colours work supremely well in the context of the gilded and richly ornamented east end elevation.

2   **Henry Holiday's** west window is a masterpiece. Completed in 1910 when Holiday was 64, it has a complex subject in which the first chapter of the Book of Genesis has been combined with the Benedicite Canticle in which the created world praises its Creator. Here God has been represented as a young man surrounded by angels and holding the firmament of Eternity. The 'Six Days of Creation' have been shown in circular medallions with 'Scenes from the Benedicite' in the spaces between. Holiday personified the elements from the Benedicte text including the 'Winds, Seas and Floods', 'Green Things', 'Showers and Wells', 'Sun, Moon', 'Night and Day.'

All are represented as beautiful expressive figures in elegant draperies. The 'Children of Men' by contrast seem rather prosaic. At the base David,

Deborah, Miriam and Moses flank Shadrach, Meshach, and Abednigo who sang the 'Benedicite' (Book of Dan) after emerging from their furnace. Indeed these figures were originally nude and Holiday was required to remove the glass and add clothes. Oddly enough the nakedness of the winds and the sexiness of most of the female figures appears to have been accepted within the canons of aesthetic taste.

3   Most of the windows installed by
Charles Eamer Kempe and Co between
1897 and 1910 were shattered during the
Blitz. However some remain on the
north side typical of the work of this
most popular of late Victorian stained
glass artists. Kempe's windows were
based on his enthusiasm for C15 Flemish
and German art. He developed a house
style for his firm in which windows were
immaculately crafted and piously tactful
in the treatment of subject. Every biblical event was illustrated in a way that
combined historical detail with a sense of
richness and comfort.

Of interest is the memorial to the Irish
poet Oliver Goldsmith which includes an
outdoors nativity scene linked with a verse
from Goldsmith's famous poem: The
Deserted Village. Ireland's 'Saint Patrick'
is the main figure dressed in a lavishly
ornamented costume with a many headed

serpent at his feet. The window includes
a clever idealised portrait of the poet.
Other Kempe windows along the north
wall commemorate distinguished
Londoners and were added between 1900
and 1920.

4 This is a rare window, the only work in glass in London by the great American artist **John La Farge**. It was made within a year of Holiday's west window. The two men knew

each others work and both had an abiding respect for classical art.

However, La Farge's training in France and his interest in the pioneering work of the Impressionists and the colour theories of Chevreul made his approach to glass much more experimental. Here Christ has been shown bending over the Jordan

River in the process of being baptised by a youthful John. Two cheerful homely angels attend the scene. The upper part of the window is entirely decorative and much repaired following bomb damage. Of considerable interest is La Farge's use of glass. Only the faces and limbs of the figures in this window have been painted, the rest has been constructed from layers of preformed glass to create an effect that the artist described as 'a translucent mosaic'. The search for the right kind of glass for this purpose led La Farge to undertake many experiments. He wanted what he called 'a degree of light and shade for each piece of glass which not only would give modelling, but also increase the depth of tone sufficiently at places to make the darker parts melt softly into the harsh lead line that binds each piece'.

13

5 The windows on the south side are all memorials. **Lawrence Lee** created a cool, rather sombre window, in memory of the Rider family to tone with those by **John Hardman** at the west end. Lee's glass is always intellectually stimulating, avoiding obvious interpretations. Here he tells the story of the building and rebuilding of the cathedral from its foundation. One of the loveliest scenes in this window shows a group of nuns being ferried across the river.

6 A memorial to Florence Tucker was added in 1993 by **Alan Younger**. He trained as a painter at the Central School of Art then worked with Carl Edwards at Blackfriars. His vision in glass developed towards abstraction in colour with symbolic associations in shape and form. He has entire control of all the processes and is particularly interested in the thoughtful modification of colour with reduction through acid etch and with the addition of paint and stain. Here, apart from the small starry faces that suggest an angelic presence, the window is concerned with colour suspended in light, the red dominant during the day and the blue taking over towards evening.

7 **Christopher Webb** won the competition held in 1954 to add a window above the fine sculpture of William Shakespeare. He created an ornamental

tree which seems to grow from the poet's memorial in whose branches the characters invented by Shakespeare could play. Prospero occupies the central window with Caliban at his feet. The comedies can be seen in the window to the left. Extracts include scenes from 'The Midsummer Nights Dream', 'Twelfth Night', 'The Merry Wives of Windsor', 'As You Like It' and 'The Merchant of Venice' The tragedies on the right include: 'Romeo and Juliet', 'Richard II', 'Richard III', 'King Lear', 'Othello', 'Macbeth' and 'Hamlet'. At the base, Webb has shown the 'Seven Ages of Man' This complex crowded window has been made accessible to the viewer by Webbs illustrative drawing and the well balanced clarity of colour.

8 **Benjamin Finn** won the competition held in 1999 to create a series of stained glass panels for the upper windows of the new Library. Finn's appealing windows combine the historical references necesary for the brief - the life of the theologian Lancelot Andrewes - with a very clear understanding of the possibilities of colour, paint and stain. These small windows are entirely fresh and add just the right note to this beautiful simple room.

Follow the river walkway past the docked ship, the Golden Hind, then pass the Clink Prison. Continue beside the Thames past the Globe Theatre, Tate Modern and Bankside Gallery. Go up steps onto Blackfriars Bridge and then left to Daily Express.

Daily Express

John Lawson of **Goddard and Gibbs** was invited to enhance the reception area with a glass feature that would bring colour into the space and provide visual entertainment for people waiting. Lawson focused on two main subjects 'Communication' on the left and 'Family Life' on the right. Both panels contain an amalgam of images, some large some small, fitted around and on top of each other - the visual equivalent of information gathered from a paper. Technically the commission was far from simple. Lawson described the chief problem as that of daylight shining through the plate glass windows onto the panels but found that he could solve this by using mirror, opac glass and lenses to gather and reflect light.

Cross Blackfriars Bridge. Exit 7 leads to Unilever House.

Unilever House

During the 1970s, Unilever commissioned **Theo Crosby** of Pentagram to
modernise their London headquarters.
Amber Hiscott was invited to design
glass for the foyer windows and those
between the exterior and interior doors.
She chose a format in tune with the

original Art Deco spirit of the building using geometric patterns derived from that period in an updated way.

She balanced the windows so that each would echo the other and chose a selection of gold, green, black and white glass to link the windows with the cladding of the interior and the greenish white of the marble floor. Hiscott was closely involved in the making of these windows at **Derix Studios** in Taunusstein in Germany, choosing the glass and arranging the complicated pattern of squares set out to symbolise the concept of structure within a multinational organisation.

Turn right and follow the curve of the building to the Embankment to reach Carmelite Street.

1 Carmelite

Both inside and out this is one of the most attractive buildings to have been added to London during the 1980s. **Brian Clarke** was invited to bring colour to the windows on the street side of the building to suggest (in a subliminal way) the connection with the nunnery once on this site. He designed a series of windows; each an entity in itself yet suggestive of sequence. These bring coloured light into the offices by day and colour the street at night. Inside, the narrative continues with a superb tapestry in Clarkes' signature

colours around the seating area in the foyer. He also designed wall hangings to carry the sense of movement to the upper floors. Indeed the interplay between the coloured glass, coloured tapestry and the sheen of the built surfaces in this unusual space is truly magical.

Walk up Carmelite to see the glass sequence. Turn right on Tudor Street to reach New Bridge Street.

100 New Bridge Street

Brian Clarke was brought into the planning of this building at an early stage with considerable success. Here colour has been used with real panache to dramatise the entrance and give a sense

of proportion to this substantial building. As in his paintings, Clarke uses the grid to suggest a sense of structure, breaking into it with a series of ribbonlike forms that lead the eye across the space.

The selected colours are bright in an entirely contemporary way - the computer age blue of the blank screen and the strange pinky reds and oranges of synthetic packaging. Only a few slices of rock inserted into the foyer glass prove that nature too can be vivid.

Walk 14

Around Hampstead and Highgate

Start: Highgate
Finish: Hampstead

Some superb glass linked by a pleasant walk across Hampstead Heath. Start early as **Evie Hone's** magnificent 'Last Supper' window can only be visited in the morning. **Burgh House** was once the home of **Thomas Grylls** co founder of the Victorian firm **Burlison and Grylls**. Memorabilia of their presence can be seen here. At **St John's Church** there are several good **Clayton and Bell** windows, an interesting window by **Ellis Wooldridge** and an **Arts and Crafts** memorial window by **Joan Fulleylove**.

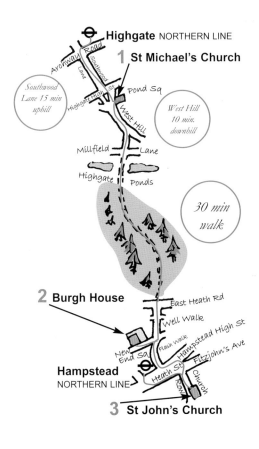

Highgate NORTHERN LINE

Aronway Road

Southwood Lane

1 St Michael's Church

Southwood Lane 15 min uphill

Highgate High St

Pond Sq

West Hill

West Hill 10 min. downhill

Millfield Lane

Highgate Ponds

30 min walk

2 Burgh House

East Heath Rd

Well Walk

Flask Walk

Hampstead High St

Fitzjohn's Ave

New End Sq

Hampstead NORTHERN LINE

Heath St

Church Row

3 St John's Church

Walk 14

Around Hampstead and Highgate

1

St Michael's Church Highgate
Pond Square
Mon - Sat 9.00 -12.00
Sunday - services only
(020) 8340 7279

2

Burgh House
New End Square
Mon - Sun 9.30 - 6.00
Closed Wed

3

St John's Church Hampstead
Church Row
Mon - Sat 10.00 - 4.00
Sunday - services only

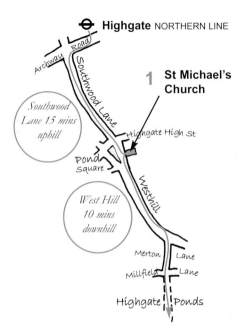

Highgate NORTHERN LINE

Archway Road

Southwood Lane

1 **St Michael's Church**

Southwood Lane 15 mins uphill

Highgate High St

Pond Square

Westhill

West Hill 10 mins downhill

Merton Lane

Millfield Lane

Highgate Ponds

Refreshments

Cafe at Burgh House. Pubs & restaurants in Highgate & Hampstead.

Walk 4

St Michael's Church, Highgate

Evie Hone's east window, the 'Last Supper', has all the power and strength that she possessed in her maturity. At first sight there is something childlike about this enormous picture, spread across the window space, in which large simplified figures have been arranged around a table. This is the second version that she made, the first being for Eton College Chapel. Here the major theme is the Supper itself with Christ at its centre blessing the bread and wine with his disciples on either side. Below, but somehow integrated into the composition, are two other events, Jesus washing Peter's feet and Judas hurrying to betray. In the traceries above, Hone has placed symbols relating to the scene below. Hone's use of colour is always uncompromising, strong and somehow right.

Walk4

There is a link with the early simplicities of medieval work and yet the effect is entirely modern.

Hone's sense of the importance of getting a colour right was described by

her friend Winifred Nicholson after a visit to her studio **An Toir Gloine** (The Glass Tower) in Dublin. 'When she was working at her windows in her high studio, she would carry heavy pieces of glass up a ladder and fix them on a window she was working at, to try them in their place, for the choice of each piece of glass was made by herself'.

Turn left on Westhill and walk over the heath towards Hampstead. Cross East Heath Road and go along Well Walk to find Burgh House.

Burgh House

During the 1870s this was the home of **John Grylls** and his numerous musical family. **Christopher Wade** who preserved this house in the form of a Trust usually has a quantity of Grylls memorabilia on display which can allow us to form some impression of the home life of the head of one of the Victorian stained glass firms. Grylls began his apprenticeship with Clayton and Bell during the 1850s where he met John Burlison. With encouragement from the parent company, the two men started their own business simply calling themselves **Burlison and Grylls**. Windows by the firm can be seen in Westminster Abbey and at Prince Henry's Room made by Harry, Thomas Grylls' son, who took over the running of the firm after his father's death.

Walk 4

St John's Church
Hampstead

This was **Alfred Bell's** local church. He
lived in a large house off Shepherd's Path
nearby and was a churchwarden here for
16 years. During the 1870s and 1880s, he

designed most of the windows in the north and south aisles, some in memory of his own children. A particularly charming window to Bell's 2 year old son Fred shows 'Christ the Good Shepherd' carrying a lost sheep while five more are grouped at his feet. Here Bell's continuing love of Medieval glass can be seen in the faux naive drawing of the figures and the crowded composition.

Two very different and much more sumptuous windows can be seen in the galleries near the chancel. These lunettes have also been based on historical antecedents. One quite clearly owes its design to Raphael's mural 'Parnassus' in the Vatican. Here Christ instructs a thoughtful group of people. The other lunette appears to be based on early Renaissance paintings in which the 'Virgin and Child' are enthroned and adored.

Here the three Kings, their attendants and horses, are somehow accompanied by maidens and shepherds bringing homely gifts. This window was used to illustrate a trade brochure sent out by the company in the 1880s.

East window

This was designed by the scholarly artist and writer **Professor Ellis Wooldridge** in 1884 and made by **Powells**. The subject is 'Christ in Glory' with 'John the Baptist' on one side and 'John the Apostle' on the other. Each has been characterised with care and all three stand within decorated arches. The glass however, appears rather flat, due - it would seem - to the effort taken by Powell's craftsmen to imitate and translate in glass and paint the full effect of Wooldridge's wonderful accurate academic drawing. Wooldridge had been trained as a painter at the Academy

Schools He designed glass for Powells
and painted murals for Watts but little
of his own work has survived.

Joan Fulleylove, another local artist, created a strange haunting war memorial
window in memory of Frederick
Haeffner who died in 1916 aged 21. She
studied painting at the Slade and then
went on to the Central School of Art to
learn stained glass and book production
with Karl Parsons and Alfred Drury.
This window was her first commission.

The scene is original in its iconography. The soldier, represented as a young
knight in armour, kneels to receive his
crown from Christ whose chiselled features, powerful neck and shadowed
downcast eyes suggest a Supreme Being
rather than the Biblical Jesus. By contrast, the angels playing instruments,
holding the knight's weapons and kneeling by the tomb seem quite suburban in
their cotton frocks and bobbed hairstyles.
At the base, the small calvary scene is
most successful. The tomb, sunset, sea and

 flowers have all been transcended by the power of Fulleylove's observation and sense of scale into a memorable image of loss and hope. The influence of the Arts and Crafts training she received can be seen in the border that runs around the edge. Here she has researched with care and painted with honesty the small tools of brutality that she wished to include, while the lettering of the inscription has been arranged in a way that uses words as the essential blocks of a composition.

End Notes

Inevitably there have been omissions. This is often because the glass is in private hands or installed in a building with a high security profile. Some good glass has quite simply been destroyed. Amber Hiscott's canopy has not been included in Liberty's makeover and Anne Smyth's panels for the booking hall of Fenchurch Street Station have been replaced by a fast food outlet. Other locations were too far out to be included within the range of this book.

Try to visit:

St Mary's Church, Battersea to see two oval windows by **James Pearson** and heraldic glass by **Bernard van Linge**. Go to **St Botolph, Aldersgate** for a superb 'Agony in the Garden' by **James Pearson**. **Christ Church, Studdridge Street** has glass by **Morris and Co** and fine windows by **Karl Parsons**. Go to **St James, Clerkenwell Close** to see a dramatic 'Ascension' window by **Heaton, Butler and Bain**.

The **Wesley Chapel** near **Old Street** contains a variety of well documented work including this 'Elijah' window by **Frank O Salisbury**. **Charing Cross Hospital, Fulham Palace Road** has 'Tree of Life' windows by **John Piper** and **Patrick Reyntiens**, also good abstract glass by **Alfred Fisher**. At **St Martins, Kensal Rise** there are fascinating Arts and Crafts windows by **Henry** and **Edward Payne**.

The text has been based on personal visits to all the buildings. Background information has been provided by the artists themselves or those who knew them well. Archival information has been obtained mostly from the Library of the Guildhall where the Faculty Papers for the installation of stained glass windows in Anglican churches can be seen. Other sources include the archive of the Council for the Care of Churches, the National Art Library at the V&A, the Library of the British Museum, Westminster Abbey Library and the archive of the Royal Institute of British Architects, The Architectural Association, the Art Worker's Guild, Sir John Soane's Museum, Linley Sambourne House and Burgh House.

An invaluable source of information for the inter and post-war years were the Journals of the British Society of Master Glass Painters, while the BSMGP magazine provided material for the 1980s and 1990s. Certain books have proved essential reading. 'Victorian Stained Glass' by Martin Harrison, 'Hints on Glass Painting' by Charles Winston, 'Art or Anti art' by John Piper, 'Stained Glass Work' by Christopher Whall, 'The Aesthetics of Stained Glass' and 'Stained Glass' by Lawrence Lee.

I would like to thank the Vicars and Vergers of the churches who tolerated my questions and gave me time to take photographs of their windows. The project has taken many years of research impossible without a grant from the Paul Mellon Centre for Studies in British Art which enabled the accumulation of the stained glass transparencies from which I have extracted the images for this book.

Elsewhere photographs have been submitted by the artists themselves (Amber Hiscott, Adelle Corrin, Graham

Jones, Alfred Fisher, Kate Maestri, Arthur
Buss, Helga Reay-Young, Benjamin Finn,
Keith New, Sally Scott) and by the kind
permission of Tim Lewis, Delmar
Flanders, Alan Powers and Martin Booth
(for Brian Clarke). The William Morris
Gallery generously waived the copyright
fee on photographs from their collection.
The Tate Gallery granted permission to
photograph and use images of their
Bossanyi window. The images relating to
the collection within the Victoria and
Albert Museum were purchased from
them. The print of the rededication of St
Olave's church first appeared in The
Times. The drawing by Dennis Flanders
(at the end) depicting Whitefriars studio
was first printed in the *Sphere*. The portrait
of Sir William Blake Richmond is in the
archive of the National Portrait Gallery.
The details of the stained glass in Lincoln's
Inn chapel come from their own archive.
The image of Joan Howson was originally
printed in the Journal of the BSMGP.

The photograph of Evie Hone first appeared in the book 'Evie Hone' published in 1958 by Browne & Nolan Ltd, Dublin. All photographs of Brian Thomas were taken as stills for a film on stained glass made at The London Film School.

Many people have helped over the years. Maureen Green, Brian Green, Jane Ewart, Jenny Morgan, Linda Lambert and students on the glass course at Central Saint Martins College of Art and Design all suggested ways in which the walks could be improved. Immensely useful advice was given by Michael Archer, Dr Hilary Wayment, Peter Cormack and Francoise Perrot. The text was read by Michael Coles whose unrivalled knowledge of London's glass alerted me to unexpected treasures (Henry Holiday's dancing girls at St Mary Magdalene, Rowington Close). Last but not least my thanks to Ginger Ferrell, a former editor of the BSMGP

magazine *Stained Glass,* whose expertise in
layout design and glass has been invaluable.
Caroline Swash

The author is the third generation of a family of stained glass artists. Her principal
windows can be seen in Gloucester and
Portsmouth Cathedrals, St Bartholomew's,
Rogate; St Paul's Church, Cleveland, Ohio
and St Barnabas, Dulwich. She currently
runs the post graduate glass courses at
Central Saint Martins College of Art and
Design.